The Emerging Laity

VOCATION, MISSION, AND SPIRITUALITY

Aurelie A. Hagstrom

Paulist Press
New York/Mahwah, NJ

A special word of thanks goes to Nancy de Flon, my editor at Paulist Press. Her wisdom, editorial acumen, and moral support helped bring this book to completion, and for that I owe her a debt of gratitude.

The Scripture quotations contained herein are from the New Revised Standard Version: Catholic Edition Copyright © 1989 and 1993, by the Division of Christian Education of the National Council of the Churches of Christ in the United States of America. Used by permission. All rights reserved.

Cover and book design by Lynn Else

Library of Congress Cataloging-in-Publication Data

Hagstrom, Aurelie A., 1963–
   The emerging laity : vocation, mission, and spirituality / Aurelie A. Hagstrom.
      p. cm.
   Includes bibliographical references.
   ISBN 978-0-8091-4652-9 (alk. paper)
   1. Laity—Catholic Church. 2. Vocation—Catholic Church. I. Title.
   BX1920.H255 2010
   262′.152—dc22

                                                            2010009724

Published by Paulist Press
997 Macarthur Boulevard
Mahwah, New Jersey 07430

www.paulistpress.com

Printed and bound in the
United States of America

Contents

To the Lay Centre at Foyer Unitas

A center of formation, dialogue, and hospitality in the heart of
Rome, where I first learned about the vocation, mission, and
spirituality of the laity.

Preface

Looking back on the twentieth century, four worldwide events stand out. Two World Wars brought devastation and death to much of the known world. In between these experiences of mass destruction was the Great Depression of the 1930s, which affected the entire world and created an atmosphere of despair as people everywhere wondered whether there would ever again be economic stability.

Then in 1962, a fourth event occurred. All the Catholic bishops from developed and developing countries gathered in Rome in response to a call from Pope John XXIII to meet in ecumenical council—the twenty-first such council in the history of the church. The reason for this extraordinary convening was to renew the church in light of contemporary needs. Pope John said he was "opening the window" to let fresh air into the church. This fresh air—new thinking, new questions, deeper understanding of tradition and truth—also ushered in, once again, the dynamism of the Holy Spirit. The Second Vatican Council brought vibrancy and hope to churches large and small. That was more than forty years ago.

Thanks to the media, successive generations have been made aware of the World Wars and the Great Depression. Films and novels and history—not to mention the political discourse of this moment—remind us of the way the world once was. The Second Vatican Council, however, has, to a great extent, been lost in time. Why? Is it because there has not been a "church version" of *Saving Private Ryan*?

The obvious reason is that in the years and decades after the council the people were actually living the renewal and reforms that flowed from four years of debate, prayer, compromise, agreement and disagreement that characterized the hard work of the council. Changes in liturgy, advances in ecumenical and interreligious relations, and the development of lay leadership soon became familiar;

what was not familiar was how the changes came to be. The density and the technical theological language of the council documents (which together, one might say, comprise the charter for change) do not render the texts "user friendly." Aurelie Hagstrom, however, does precisely that in *The Emerging Laity*.

While carefully presenting the scriptural and historical foundations regarding the place and role of ordinary people in the church—which is to say, the 99 percent who are not ordained—she does so in language that is direct, accessible, and unencumbered. There is, indeed, a dynamism in rendering the story of the council and its call to laity to *be* the church in the world and also to assume responsibility within. This dynamism is a reflection of the fact that the central player in *The Emerging Laity* is the Holy Spirit, who is not static and never confined. The Spirit is everywhere, in baptism and mission, in the details of ordinary daily life, indwelling in each one of us and in the community. Dr. Hagstrom makes this abundantly clear.

The Emerging Laity may not be the theological answer to *Saving Private Ryan*, but, unlike the fictional Private Ryan, it tells a true story. As such it is a major resource for all the People of God to remember—or to learn for the first time—how and why the laity have moved to the center of the church's life in the years following the Second Vatican Council.

Dolores R. Leckey
Woodstock Theological Center

Introduction

"Why haven't we heard this before? It's been more than forty years since Vatican II. Why is this teaching such a well-kept secret?"

I hear these questions nearly everywhere I go when I present the teaching of the Second Vatican Council on the vocation, mission, and spirituality of the laity. It seems that the call and role of the layperson in the church and in the world are still not very well known by ordinary Catholics. This book presents the teaching of Vatican II, along with some more recent documents regarding the laity, in a simple way so that lay men and women might understand who they are in the church and what God has called them to do. Indeed, the council issued a sort of "wake-up" call to the laity—and it's time they woke up!

The teachings of Vatican II are still not very well known by Catholics at the grassroots level because the sixteen documents produced by the council are not exactly beach reading. At times they can be difficult to understand for those who do not have a background in the study of theology and church teaching. While some of the passages of the conciliar documents are certainly inspirational and can cause the spirit to soar, the overall language and style used by the council fathers can be somewhat impenetrable and confusing for nonspecialists.

My goal in this book, having studied these texts for over twenty years, is to translate the Second Vatican Council's theology of the laity into simple and clear language for others who have not made such a serious study. The many talks, workshops, courses, and seminars that I have given over the years to lay women and men at parishes, schools, and conferences have helped me tremendously in this effort. These experiences in the trenches have greatly benefited my teaching and scholarly reading and research. My pastoral experiences among other ordinary

Catholics have enabled me to read the documents of Vatican II at even deeper levels.

The questions, insights, and Christian witness of the lay men and women at my presentations over the years have been great gifts to me. And so I am writing this book to help laypersons to perceive their ordinary lives as part of God's wonderful plan to bring about the transformation of the world and the salvation of all. The Christian adventure of the Catholic laity includes a vocation, mission, and spirituality. In my experience, once laypeople are introduced to the church's teaching in these areas, it gives them a tremendous freedom and joy. They realize that holiness is not beyond their reach and that their daily lives are infused with God's presence, if they only have eyes to see and ears to hear.

Structure of the Book

The book consists of six chapters. Chapter one discusses the surprising call for a council by Pope John XXIII in 1959 and introduces some basic ideas of how the church's thinking on the laity unfolded during Vatican II. Chapter two begins the more formal theological analysis and highlights the notion of the lay vocation in the council documents and in the 1988 apostolic exhortation of Pope John Paul II, *Christifideles Laici,* On the Vocation and Mission of the Lay Faithful in the Church and in the World. God's call comes to all believers first of all through baptism. This new life that flows from baptism is one of discipleship and ongoing conversion. And for the laity, the experience of vocation is shaped by their deep engagement in the life of the world. Therefore, chapter two also introduces the concept of the secular character of the laity.

Chapter three unpacks the universal call to holiness from Vatican II. This New Testament exhortation to holiness is one of the key features of the council's teaching on the spiritual lives of all believers, and it had a huge impact on the laity. Holiness is not just for a select few in the church, but is the common call of all the baptized, although lived out in a variety of ways. This chapter explains the basics of the reality of holiness in the Bible and then applies it to the daily lives of lay men and women.

The participation of the laity in the mission of the church is the subject of chapter four. One of the reasons why holiness is not optional or an extra for the lives of believers is that the mission of the church depends on holiness. Holiness, union with God in charity, is the spiritual energy source needed for mission. Chapter four explores how the Holy Spirit is given in baptism and confirmation to energize the laity for their participation in Christ's mission to transform the world.

The council fathers of Vatican II did not consider the responsibility for the mission of the church as being given only to the clergy and religious. Instead they challenged the laity to see themselves as being personally commissioned by Christ to share in his work of redemption. Since an important part of this commissioning is the reception of the gifts of the Holy Spirit, chapter four treats the subject of charisms. These gifts of the Holy Spirit are given to the laity to build up the life of the church and to enable them to be witnesses for Christ in the world through their ordinary lives and activities.

This one mission of Christ is expressed in a diversity of ways in the lives of laypersons. Chapter five is about the ministry of the laity within the church. Vatican II taught that some lay women and men can be called to a closer collaboration with the hierarchy in various ministries, according to the needs of the faithful. These more formal ways of participating in ministry have expanded rapidly in the forty-plus years since the council. Lay men and women have come to fulfill roles within the church that were previously considered the sole responsibility of the clergy.

This explosion of lay ministries in the church after the council is really not something new; rather, it is a revival of the notion of shared ministry found in the New Testament. St. Paul names many coworkers who labored with him in a Spirit-filled, collaborative way in the ministry of the Gospel. And Vatican II appeals to this experience of St. Paul and the early Christians in its understanding of how the laity can be called to formal ministry within the inner life of the church. Chapter five also introduces *Co-Workers in the Vineyard of the Lord*, the document on the theology of lay ecclesial ministry published by the United States Conference of Catholic Bishops in 2005.

Chapter six is about the spirituality that is the foundation of the vocation, mission, and ministry of the laity. This final chapter focuses on the building blocks for a lay spirituality coming from the teachings of Vatican II. While the council did not offer a full-blown treatment of the spirituality of lay men and women, it did suggest certain fundamental components that should be found in the spiritual life of any Christian. These building blocks include the word of God, sacraments, prayer, charisms or gifts of the Holy Spirit, virtues, Christian friendships, associations, and love of God and neighbor.

The council fathers did not accept a "one-size-fits-all" under-standing of Christian spirituality. Therefore the shape of the spir-ituality of lay men and women will fit the contours of their daily lives, relationships, work, activities, and sufferings. The great chal-lenge for the laity is to overcome the false dichotomy between their "real lives" and their "spiritual lives." Ordinary affairs and the messiness of the mundane are not distractions from the Christian journey of the laity; on the contrary, it is precisely amidst the rough and tumble of family life and work commitments that their growth in holiness takes place.

Vatican II and St. Paul

One thing that should become clear as the book unfolds is my conviction that the teaching of St. Paul is an integral part of the council's thinking on the church. Put simply, I contend that Vatican II reclaimed the early Pauline theology of the church and that the result of this was a renewed theology of the laity. By reappropriating St. Paul's ecclesiology, his theology of baptism, and his theology of charisms, Vatican II was able to rebalance the Catholic understanding of the identity and function of the laity in the church.

St. Paul had been somewhat neglected in Catholic ecclesi-ology since the sixteenth-century Reformation, in my opinion. Martin Luther and the Reformers were studying St. Paul, preaching St. Paul, and attempting to reform the church according to their interpretations of St. Paul's insights in the New Testament. The Protestant Reformers stressed St. Paul's theology of grace, his emphasis on charisms, and his focus on baptism, among other components of his teachings.

It seems to me that Protestantism is "Pauline," and we might say that Catholicism reacted to the Reformation by becoming almost exclusively "Petrine." That is, Catholicism is focused very much on the person, legacy, and office of St. Peter, the papacy, the power of the sacraments, hierarchy, and the primacy of Rome in Christianity—the "Petrine," in other words. It took nearly four hundred years for Catholicism to reclaim St. Paul back into our theology. The Pauline and the Petrine dimensions of the church were finally reunited, as it were, at Vatican II.

It seemed providential, therefore, that it was at the tomb of St. Paul in 1959 that Pope John XXIII called for an ecumenical council. There, at the sacred site of devotion to St. Paul, Pope John XXIII dropped his bombshell of an announcement to the astonished cardinals and Roman Curia gathered there for the Pauline feast. Was it merely a coincidence that the tomb of St. Paul the Apostle was the place for this papal announcement? Not in my opinion. The Holy Spirit was at work! Vatican II invited St. Paul back into the conversation about the church and in so doing renewed the theology of the vocation and mission of the laity. Welcome home, St. Paul!

Pope Benedict XVI and the Pauline Year

Nearly fifty years after Pope John XXIII issued his call for a Second Vatican Council at St. Paul's tomb, Pope Benedict XVI inaugurated a Pauline Year on June 28, 2008. In his homily during the celebration of First Vespers of the Solemnity of Peter and Paul, at the basilica of St. Paul-Outside-the-Walls, Pope Benedict XVI convoked the Pauline Jubilee, which extended until June 29, 2009. "We are gathered before the tomb of St. Paul, who was born 2,000 years ago in Tarsus of Cilicia," the pope said, "[however], we have come together not to reflect on a past history, irrevocably surpassed. Paul wants to speak to us today." The reason why the pope convoked the Pauline Jubilee year was so that the church could "listen to him and to drink from him, as our teacher in the faith and truth, in which are rooted the reasons for unity among the disciples of Christ...."

The pope referred to St. Paul as "our teacher, apostle, and herald of Jesus Christ" who can speak to the church today. Therefore the question of the Pauline Jubilee is not: Who was St. Paul? Instead, as the pope insisted, "Above all, we ask ourselves 'Who is Paul?' 'What is he saying to me?' " (Pope Benedict XVI, Homily, First Vespers of the Solemnity of the Holy Apostles Peter and Paul, June 28, 2008).

Indeed, St. Paul still challenges and exhorts the church today—from his New Testament writings right up through the documents of Vatican II and beyond that convey his teachings. For the purposes of this book on the laity, perhaps most helpful is his grasp of the mystery of the church. His conversion experience on the road to Damascus (Acts 9:3–8) contains a deep insight about the church. When the risen Lord tells St. Paul, "I am Jesus, whom you are persecuting," he identifies the church with himself. The Christians whom St. Paul was persecuting were to be identified with Jesus himself. This statement of Jesus to St. Paul contains within it the whole doctrine of the church as the Body of Christ. More than just an analogy, for St. Paul, "Body of Christ" is about perceiving the person of the risen Lord with his followers as a single subject.

The New Pentecost

When lay men and women can perceive themselves as members of the Body of Christ, in union with the person of the risen Lord, then the renewal generated by Vatican II takes shape. Pope John XXIII expressed his hope for the council with the phrase *new Pentecost*. He was not hoping for a brand-new church or even a refounding of the church. Rather, he was praying for a fresh outpouring of the Holy Spirit to energize the church's mission to renew the face of the earth. In a particular way, this book attempts to explain how the laity were, and continue to be, affected by this new Pentecost to which Vatican II gave rise. By yielding to the power of the Holy Spirit, lay men and women will be able to live out their vocation, fulfill their mission, and grow in their spirituality of intimacy with the risen Lord.

CHAPTER ONE

The Second Vatican Council and the Laity

The Surprising Call for a Council

On January 25, 1959, the Feast of the Conversion of St. Paul, something almost totally unexpected happened: the newly elected pope, John XXIII, announced his intention to summon an ecumenical council for the worldwide church. The pope, along with the cardinals of Rome and the Roman Curia, had just finished celebrating Mass together at the basilica of St. Paul-Outside-the-Walls in Rome. Usually it is the custom for the pope to give a short speech after the Mass to the assembly gathered there at the tomb of St. Paul the Apostle. And it was then that the pope issued his surprising call for a council.

It is said that Pope John XXIII's audience met his startling announcement with stunned silence and disbelief. Why should there be an ecumenical council? There had not been a church council for nearly one hundred years, and the church was experiencing no discernable crisis. In the past, councils were usually called in response to problems within the church or in response to heresies challenging the faith of the church. But in the middle of the twentieth century, the church seemed to be in a very strong position.

If the absence of any major crisis in the church was one reason that made the pope's announcement surprising, then another reason why it came as such a shock was the person of the pope himself. When Angelo Roncalli was elected to be Pope John XXIII, he was widely seen as a transitional pope. After the long reign of Pope Pius XII, the cardinals wanted a short period of stability and tranquility during which they could choose a successor who would also have a long pontificate. They expected the seventy-seven-year-old Angelo Roncalli, Pope John XXIII, only to "keep the Chair of Peter warm" until another younger, more energetic man could be found. No one thought that Pope John XXIII would rock the boat or change the status quo of the church. Therefore, he surprised everyone when, less than a year into his pontificate, he announced that he was summoning an ecumenical council—Vatican II.

In spite of the general reaction of surprise, Pope John XXIII was convinced that God wanted a council. The Second Vatican Council opened on October 11, 1962. In his opening message, Pope John set the tone for the drama that was about to unfold. One main theme of his stirring speech was that the council must bring the church "up to date." When asked by a reporter what he expected from the council, Pope John replied that he wanted to "open the windows of the Vatican" and let "a breath of fresh air into the church."

Something quite new was going on with Pope John XXIII's vision. Clearly, the pope's desire to update the church reflected an optimism about the modern world that was a departure from the convictions of most of his recent predecessors. He regarded the modern world not as the enemy of the church, but rather as the very place in which God was working out his plan for the salvation of the human race. The boldness of Pope John XXIII's vision was reflected in his desire that the council would not only address Catholics, but also that it would have something to say to the entire world about the relevancy of Christ and the Gospel to men and women of the modern age.

The pope's opening message also emphasized that this was to be a pastoral rather than a dogmatic council. That is, this council would not focus on developing new doctrine, but would find better ways of expressing and communicating traditional church teaching. Pope John XXIII wanted to engage the minds and hearts of modern men and women with the good news of the Gospel in a way that would speak to their needs, questions, and aspirations. The language of the documents of Vatican II was to be, therefore, neither negative nor defensive, but rather positive and pastoral. In this way, according to the pope, the church would "meet the needs of the present day more by demonstrating the validity of her teaching than by condemnation."

A New Pentecost

The Second Vatican Council has been called "a new Pentecost" in the life of the church. In fact, Pope John XXIII urged Catholics the world over to pray for the success of the council by asking God for a new Pentecost, a fresh outpouring of the Holy Spirit that would renew the face of the earth. His suggested prayer was:

> Divine Spirit, renew your wonders in this our age as in a new Pentecost, and grant that your Church, praying perseveringly and insistently with one heart and mind together with Mary, the Mother of Jesus, and guided by blessed Peter, may increase the reign of the Divine Savior, the reign of truth and justice, the reign of love and peace. Amen.[1]

The sixteen documents produced by the council bear the fruits of this prayer. Each one addresses a different topic in the life of the church. Their teachings are both a retrieval of ancient doctrine and a renewed application of Christian truths to modern questions and issues.

The "wind and fire" of this new Pentecost has been experienced most keenly, perhaps, by the lay faithful in the church. Prior to Vatican II, the laity had not been the specific subject of conciliar teaching for four hundred years—since the Council of Trent. This renewed teaching on the laity has produced numerous publications, conferences, debates, and discussions concerning the vocation and mission of the laity. Indeed, during the forty-plus years since the close of the council, Catholics have witnessed an ongoing deepening of the theological understanding of the laity. Some of the fruits of the Spirit that have resulted from Vatican II's teaching have been: a deeper appreciation and emphasis on the fundamental equality and dignity of the lay faithful as members of the Body of Christ, their share in the mission of the church, the significance of their call to holiness, and the sacramental grounding of their vocation and mission. This tremendous work of the Holy Spirit in regard to the laity can perhaps be more fully appreciated when we consider the role of the laity in the church before Vatican II.

The Call to Adulthood in the Church

It is not an exaggeration to say that in many ways the church hierarchy treated the laity like children in the past. The church leadership did not view laypeople as capable of exercising any significant role, since they had no expertise in church matters. Thus the hierarchy entertained extremely low expectations for the lay vocation and mission. They considered laypersons to be incapable of initiative in many areas of parish or diocesan life. Treated as children, the lay faithful up to this point in time were chiefly to "be seen and not heard." This meant that the voice of the laity was not usually required or appreciated in discussions concerning church teaching, policies, or practice. The traditional relationship between the clergy and the laity resembled that between a responsible, all-knowing parent and a dependent, ignorant child.

Among other insights, the Second Vatican Council brought a renewed vision of the church as the Body of Christ and the People of God. This New Testament understanding of the church called lay men and women to adulthood and challenged them to assume a more mature identity and role. No longer patronized as dependent children, laypeople were exhorted to take on their dignity and equality as members of the church. According to the council fathers, "The Laity are called to participate actively in the whole life of the church; not only are they to animate the world with the spirit of Christianity, but they are to be witnesses to Christ in all circumstances and at the very heart of the community of mankind."[2]

With the call to adulthood came a new appreciation for the wisdom and knowledge that the laity potentially bring to church issues. The wisdom derived from family life, work, political engagement, and community involvement was now not only affirmed but also sought after in the life of the church.

Laymen should also know that it is generally the function of their well-formed Christian conscience to see that the divine law is inscribed in the life of the earthly city; from priests they may look for spiritual light and nourishment. Let the layman not imagine that his pastors are always such experts, that to every problem which arises, however complicated, they can readily give him a concrete solution, or even that such is their mission. Rather, enlightened by Christian wisdom and giving close attention to the teaching authority of the Church, let the layman take on his own distinctive role. (GS 43)

The Universal Call to Holiness

Since the days of the apostles, Christians have been called to holiness of life. The reality of holiness, in fact, goes back to the Old Testament and the experience of the ancient Jews. God entered into a covenant with his people and made it clear that he expected them to be holy as he is holy. The early church adopted this theme as a basic component of its life. Baptized Christians were to be holy in every dimension of their lives. "Instead, as he who called you is holy, be holy yourselves in all your conduct; for it is written, 'You shall be holy, for I am holy' " (1 Pet 1:15–16).

As the centuries of the church unfolded, however, this call to holiness seemed to become directed at only a minority in the church. Laypeople were usually not seriously expected to be holy. Since the laity lived "in the world" and were concerned with "worldly affairs," their potential to be holy was thought to be limited at best. This way of thinking regarded lay men and women as somehow tainted by their engagement with family life and work and these daily concerns and responsibilities as a distraction from the spiritual life.

The very notion of holiness became distorted and the rich biblical tradition was nearly lost. Holiness was available to clergy and vowed religious, but hardly to anyone else, because holiness became associated with the clerical and religious life. The three vows of poverty, chastity, and obedience were considered nearly a prerequisite for living an intense faith life. The clerical and religious vocations were predisposed for heroic sanctity because they were "otherworldly." Freed from the distractions and temptations of daily lay life, these religious and clerical elite were held up as models of true Christian living. Since holiness became focused on the performance of religious duties and rituals, living a lay life in the world seemed to preclude one from ever achieving it. Of course, the laity were encouraged to live a life of piety and devotion, but expectations were low because of their commitments of marriage, children, work, and other nonreligious affairs.

The New Testament understanding of the church revived by Vatican II exposed these distortions in the reality of holiness as the council fathers once again emphasized the biblical concept of all believers being called to holiness. Since there are no distinctions among believers in their common call to holiness, then the church should not create first-, second-, or third-class notions of holiness. Vatican II emphasized that those who embrace the clerical and religious vocations are not automatically holier than other baptized believers. Celibacy is not necessarily holier than marriage, and the daily affairs of the lives of the laity have just as much challenge for holiness as the formal religious duties of clergy, nuns, and monks. This universal call to holiness is one of the most exciting elements in the theology of the laity from the council.

> The classes and duties of life are many, but holiness is one—that sanctity which is cultivated by all who are moved by the Spirit of God, and who obey the voice of the Father and worship God the Father in spirit and in truth....Every person must walk unhesitatingly according to his own personal gifts and duties in the path of living faith, which arouses hope and works through charity....Finally all Christ's faithful, whatever be the conditions, duties and circumstances of their lives— and indeed through all these, will daily increase in holiness, if they receive all things with faith from the hand of their heavenly Father and if they cooperate with the divine will.[3]

Pay, Pray, and Obey

Before Vatican II revived the New Testament vision of the church, it was quite common to think of the church in political terms. That is, the church was described as an unequal society. In an equal society, all the members have equal status, dignity, and rights. Put simply, the clergy had the power of authority and the laity did not. Only the clergy were empowered to teach, sanctify, and govern the rest of the faithful. This image goes back centuries and was even ingrained in the 1917 Code of Canon Law. This code had hardly any laws or canons concerning the laity besides those regulating the sacrament of marriage.

Before the 1960s, then, theological teaching about the church and church law focused on the identity of the clergy and the structure of the hierarchy. Within this unequal society, the lay faithful were by and large excluded from the church's mission or apostolate and were regarded as appendages to the church with little to no role to play. They were defined solely by their involvement in the affairs of the world, rather than by their membership in the Body of Christ through baptism. The unequal society model emphasized the functions of the laity in the world, without a corresponding emphasis on their activities within the church.

This approach, which practically lost sight of the lay faithful, took for granted that the church was the domain of the clergy. It did not appreciate the mission of the laity, since the power in the church was concentrated in the office of the pope and the hierarchy. Instead, the implicit identity that this unequal society model gave the laity was one of docility and passiveness. Laypeople were to "pay, pray, and obey," and simply allow themselves to be led like a docile flock by the pastors of the church. They were to express their fidelity to the church by following the pastors like sheep follow a shepherd. This misuse of the biblical metaphor of shepherding unfortunately placed the laity into a state of nearly total passivity when it came to the mission of the church.

Vatican II reclaimed the notion that the mission of the church is the responsibility of all of its members. There are to be no purely passive members of the Body of Christ. Baptism calls everyone to fulfill the mission of Christ, which is "to spread the kingdom of Christ throughout the earth for the glory of God the Father, to enable all men to share in His saving redemption, and that through them the whole world might enter into a relationship with Christ...." In this baptismal call, "...there is a diversity of ministry but a oneness of mission...the laity have therefore, in the church and in the world, their own assignment in the mission of the whole people of God."[4]

One Mission, Many Ministries

The church's teaching on mission and ministry evolved at the council. Previously, as seen above, the laity were not considered to be responsible for the mission of the church. And certainly no serious theological discussion about laypersons exercising any ministries within the life of the church had taken place before this. At best, lay men and women were invited to "help Father" or "help Sister" in some work of apostolate or ministry. Theology and church law taught that ministries within the church were only entrusted to the ordained clergy. All other members of the church were the passive recipients of that clerical ministry.

One reason why the laity were not expected to engage in ministries within the life of the church was that they were defined exclusively by their activities in the world. Because the lay faithful lived in the world, worked jobs, raised children, and were generally occupied with mundane affairs, they were considered to be excluded from the sacred ministries inside the church. Put simply, by their ordination the clergy were directed to ministry within the church while the laity were directed to life in the world. The activities of the clergy were "sacred" whereas the daily affairs of the laity were "profane."

This is not, however, to say that no opportunities for lay action existed in the earlier decades of the twentieth century. Lay associations such as the Legion of Mary, the Knights of Columbus, or Catholic Action had members that were involved in parish and diocesan life. This involvement, however, was considered to be a "sharing in the apostolate of the hierarchy" and not an independent lay ministry. Members of Catholic Action, for example, were described as the "right arm of the hierarchy in the world." Anything resembling the lay apostolate before the Second Vatican Council had to be organized, mandated, and controlled by the clergy.

The discussions at the council opened the door for a fuller participation of the laity in the inner life of the church. The result has been a virtual explosion of lay ministries over the past forty years since the council. This recent phenomenon of ecclesial lay ministers in the church has its beginnings in the conciliar teaching that the sacraments of baptism and confirmation equip lay women and men for any ministry (AA 3). The council fathers even acknowledge a certain autonomy of the laity in selected apostolic endeavors (AA 24).

Church vs. World?

One final factor that shaped the traditional view of the laity was the common perception that existed concerning the Christian attitude toward the "world." Since the earliest days of the church there has been a strain of thinking that has characterized the world as evil and spiritually dangerous. This belief stemmed from a particular reading of John's gospel and its use of the term *world* for anyone who was opposed to Jesus and his message. The thinking was that since the devil was the prince of the world, believers should be careful not to be involved in the "affairs of the world." Jesus, after all, called the devil the "prince of this world" and said that he had called his followers "out from the world" (see John 12 and 15). In fact, Jesus even warns his followers that the "world will hate them" (John 15:18–19).

From a misunderstanding of these New Testament texts and others there developed a simplistic notion of the church being in opposition to the world. The world was a kind of battlefield between the forces of truth and falsehood, good and evil, light and darkness. Christians should therefore avoid engagement with the world as much as possible. The best stance toward the world for Christians was one of contempt. Holiness became defined as a state of other-worldliness and the laity, as seen above, were regarded as living a compromised life in the world as a concession to human weakness. Because they lived in the secular world, their lives could not be considered sacred, since the world could only be a source of temptations and distractions.

The teaching of Vatican II challenged this centuries-old contempt for the world held by some Christians. Grounding itself in biblical passages like Genesis 1 and John 3, the council affirmed the basic goodness of the world. Since God created the world and called it "good," he loves the world and even sent his son Jesus into the world as savior and redeemer.

> Therefore...the world...is the theater of man's history, and the heir of his energies, his tragedies and his triumphs; that world which the Christian sees as created and sustained by its Maker's love, fallen indeed into the bondage of sin, yet emancipated now by Christ, Who was crucified and rose again to break the strangle hold of personified evil, so that the world might be fashioned anew according to God's design and reach its fulfillment. (GS 2)

This positive vision of the world has had a profound impact on the reality of lay spirituality. Since the laity are intimately involved in the affairs of the world, this context must be taken into account in any attempts to form a lay spirituality. Recognizing the spiritual potential of secular activity, the council calls upon the faithful to learn the value of all creation, to acknowledge its role in the praise of God, and to help one another to grow in holiness even in their daily occupations (LG 36).

The daily, ordinary lives of the laity are actually the very stuff or fodder of the Christian life. It is precisely in the midst of family life, work, politics, business, education, science, the arts, leisure time, community involvement, and so forth, that lay men and women hear the call to holiness. These activities are to be considered not as obstacles or hindrances to the spiritual life, but rather as opportunities to receive God's grace and to grow in holiness. The council fathers make it clear that "all their works, prayers and apostolic endeavors, their ordinary married and family life, their daily occupations, their physical and mental relaxation, if carried out in the Spirit, and even the hardships of life, if patiently borne—all these become 'spiritual sacrifices acceptable to God through Jesus Christ'" (LG 34).

Breakthroughs in the Theology of the Laity

This brief survey of the traditional state of the laity makes it clear that a change in the theology and church practice involving the lay faithful was sorely needed. The renewed vision of the life of the church, as expressed by the council, was a true movement of the Holy Spirit. The new Pentecost for which Pope John XXIII prayed resulted in a reinvigoration of the life of the church on every level. But it was perhaps the lay faithful who experienced the most profound changes in the understanding of their identity and role.

The call to adulthood challenged lay women and men to take up their rightful role and claim their full dignity as members of the Body of Christ. Instead of the low expectations that the hierarchy seemed to have had regarding the laity in the past, now the council was exhorting laypeople to maturity in the practice of their faith. They were no longer to be seen as dependent children without expertise or unworthy of serious consultation concerning church matters. On the contrary, the wisdom that comes from ordinary family life, work, and daily experiences is to be valued and sought after.

The universal call to holiness issued by Vatican II also had a profound impact on the faith life of the laity. Instead of trying to get to heaven on the coattails of the clergy or religious, now laypersons were to cultivate their own holiness right in the midst of the rhythms of their daily lives. No longer was it the case that only the religious elite could be heroic in sanctity. All members of the church could grow closer to Christ, not just those living the three religious vows of poverty, chastity, and obedience. New models of holiness were to include ordinary lay men and women who lived their baptism intensely and were dynamic witnesses to Christ in the world.

In the wake of the Second Vatican Council, the prevailing model of the church shifted from that of the unequal society to a biblical model of People of God, Body of Christ, or communion of the faithful. This shift prodded Catholic laypeople to abandon their passive sheep mentality and challenged them to assume the full share in the mission of Christ that was theirs by reason of their baptism and confirmation. This responsibility included taking the initiative in certain areas of the church's life and work.

Within the one mission of the church there exist a variety of ministries, and the council fathers taught that laypeople can even participate in certain formal sacred ministries previously reserved for those who were ordained to the priesthood. Empowered by the gifts they received in baptism and confirmation, the lay faithful exercise certain ministries in the inner life of the church to build up and strengthen the entire communion of the faithful. The council also urged that participation in these ministries is to be done in a spirit of mutual collaboration with the clergy.

Finally, the more positive and optimistic view of the world promoted by Vatican II affirmed the lay life. This approach to the world, based in Christian hope, put a new value on the ordinary activities, duties, and commitments of laypeople. Lay spirituality embraces the very stuff of their worldly responsibilities, which became viewed as opportunities for rather than distractions from spiritual growth. And the spiritual life of the laity, rather than being a watered-down version of the spirituality of priests, monks, or nuns, should take its own form, shape, and expression according to the lived experience of laypeople themselves.

Conclusion

Indeed, the Second Vatican Council ushered in a new Pentecost for the laity. In fact, the very first line of the very first conciliar document published described the chief aim of the council, which was "to impart an ever increasing vigor to the Christian life of the faithful."[5] Certainly, the lives of the laity were invigorated and stirred up by all of the breakthroughs mentioned in this chapter.

In many ways, the church is still "unpacking" the insights, teachings, and directives of the council fathers. The Holy Spirit continues to lead the church into all truth, as Christ promised:

"When the Spirit of truth comes, he will guide you into all the truth" (John 16:13). And so the ongoing prayer of the church must be for the inspiration and guidance of the Spirit of Pentecost.

> Come, Holy Spirit, fill the hearts of your faithful and kindle in us the fire of your love. Send forth your Spirit and we shall be recreated. And you will renew the face of the earth. Let us pray: O God, who did instruct the hearts of your faithful people by the light of your Holy Spirit, grant that by the same Spirit we may be truly wise and ever rejoice in his consolation. We ask this through Jesus Christ our Lord. Amen.

Reflection Questions

1. How would you describe the historical importance of the Second Vatican Council for Catholics?

2. What are the challenges implied in the call to adulthood for the laity?

3. How does the notion of "the world" influence your understanding of holiness?

4. How have you experienced the new Pentecost of Vatican II in your own life or parish experience?

CHAPTER TWO

The Call or Vocation of the Laity

Who Are the Laity?

During the discussions among the bishops at the Second Vatican Council, one important issue that surfaced was the description of the various members of the church. If the council fathers desired to move away from the notion of the church as an unequal society, then what was an effective way to name the different vocations in the church? These discussions about identity were critically important because the council wanted to use a language that would inspire and motivate all members of the church to embrace their vocations and live a more intense Christian life. Finding a renewed way of speaking about the church was one of the ways the council hoped to promote renewal in its life and mission.

When the discussions came around to the topic of the lay faithful, the council fathers had to contend with centuries of theology that usually marginalized the laity. Before Vatican II, most of the church's teaching and law concerning vocations assumed that *vocation* referred to clergy and religious. Therefore the bishops did not have much material to work with, and the material that they did have was usually negative in tone.

In the past, the description of the laity had been framed in negative language—that is, in terms of what they were *not*. Laypeople were *not* clergy and they were *not* vowed religious. To describe people as "not" is hardly the best way of helping them to have a strong sense of their identity and dignity. In this unequal society, the laity were described as a class over against the clergy or a class over against religious. This negative view regarded lay women and men as people who existed by virtue of a concession to weakness—that is, they did not live the three religious vows of poverty, chastity, and obedience. Instead, they lived worldly lives and were usually married. This negative approach to describing the laity usually resulted in a division between the church and the world, the sacred and the profane. Spiritual things belonged to the clergy and religious while worldly or profane things pertained to the laity. The laity therefore had no role, responsibility, or power in the inner life of the church.

In some ways it might have been a good thing that there was not a very well developed theology of the lay vocation before Vatican II. In this way, the Holy Spirit could inspire the council to do something new. The time was ripe for a mature thinking on the dignity of the lay vocation. The new Pentecost of Vatican II could produce a way of speaking about the laity that was grounded in the New Testament and yet open to the modern experiences of laypeople themselves. The council's solution was to reclaim the dignity of the call of baptism: to get beyond the negative perception of the lay vocation by highlighting the New Testament teaching that baptism is the center and source of every vocation in the life of the church.

Defining *laity* as all the faithful "except those in holy orders and those in the state of religious life specially approved by the Church," the council fathers declared baptism to be the means by which the lay faithful are incorporated into the people of God and come to share in the priestly, prophetical, and kingly offices of Christ. They are thus empowered to "carry out for their own part the mission of the whole people in the Church and in the world" (LG 31).

Putting Baptism Back into the Center

One of the reasons for the negative description of the laity in the past was that the point of reference for all church membership was the sacrament of priesthood or holy orders. Since the church had been described as if the center of its life was the sacrament of holy orders, everyone else in the church was considered in reference to the clergy. Instead of a theology of the church, with its various members and vocations, there emerged a theology of the priesthood and hierarchy. The theology of the church really became a theology of holy orders. The duties, responsibilities, and powers of the hierarchy formed the center of the teaching on church membership. If the church community was regarded as a wheel, the hub of that wheel was holy orders. The other sacraments and vocations were simply spokes that emanated from the hub of the clergy. No wonder the lay vocation seemed peripheral.

The Second Vatican Council put baptism back into the center of our theology of the church. As the most fundamental identity of any member of the church, baptism and not holy orders is the starting point for any consideration of vocations. The call and identity of all the baptized is the norm, and all other Christian vocations must be regarded in relation to it. This is clearly taught in the New Testament and was reclaimed by the council. The theology of the church as formulated by the council fathers moved away from the old division of making the clergy "sacred" while the laity were "only secular." Instead, it viewed all vocations as flowing from the foundation of baptism. Certainly, the vocation of the clergy is of fundamental importance to the church, but it is founded on the sacrament of baptism. In fact, the clergy need to be described in relation to the laity, and not vice-versa.

By describing the church as the Body of Christ, the people of God, or the communion of the faithful, Vatican II affirmed the fundamental dignity and equality of every vocation. The common foundation of the whole church is the baptismal identity of each member. Indeed, the spiritual dynamism or grace for any vocation is grounded in the reality of baptism. This recentering of the theology of the church promoted a more positive view of the laity and their place in the community of the faithful. Through baptism all the faithful share a common dignity as members of the people of God, as well as the same call to perfection (LG 32).

The positive view of the laity that resulted from highlighting baptism contrasts starkly with the former way of speaking about the church. The unequal society model resulted in a sort of power-pyramid understanding of the church. The various vocations in the church were arranged in a pyramid, with the pope and hierarchy at the top and the laity at the bottom. Power exercised within the church flowed from the top of the pyramid. Although the majority of the members of the church were at the base of the pyramid, the duties, rights, and responsibilities for the inner life of the church were concentrated at the top. This left the laity in the old "pay, pray, and obey" mode.

Instead of the power pyramid, the Second Vatican Council presented a view of the church as a communion of members with a common dignity, common identity, and common call to holiness, all flowing from a common baptism. While this is a more horizontal view of the church than the old unequal society model, it does not erase the distinctive identities of the various vocations or states of life that flow from baptism, namely, the laity, religious, and clergy. It does, however, make clear that the most fundamental identity of anyone in the church is the identity that comes from baptism. Although there are different vocations, all share the same call to holiness and enjoy true equality regarding the dignity and the activity "common to all the faithful for the building up of the Body of Christ." All the faithful, then, "bear witness to the wonderful unity in the Body of Christ. This very diversity of graces, ministries and works gathers the children of God into one, because 'all these things are the work of one and the same Spirit'" (LG 32).

With the power pyramid, in effect, turned upside down, the starting point of church identity becomes baptism and the common membership in the people of God. The base of the pyramid, the laity, becomes the point of departure for understanding the other vocations in the church. The vocations of the clergy and religious must be explained in relation to the laity, and not vice-versa. The power and graces of baptism are what energize any roles, ministries, or activities in the life of the church.

What is remarkable about the council's shift in the understanding of the church is that it is really not new; in fact, it comes from the New Testament. The council did not have to construct a new interpretation of baptism in its efforts to describe the laity in a positive way; instead, it reclaimed the experience of the early Christians and their community life. The texts of the New Testament present an understanding of the church as neither an unequal society nor a power pyramid. And it is this New Testament vision of the church that Vatican II reclaimed. The renewal of the life of the laity brought about by the council was really due to a deeper appreciation for the ancient theology of the church coming from the early Christians and the New Testament.

The Church as a Communion

One of the key elements in the teachings of the Second Vatican Council is that the church is a communion. This concept is found in the writings of St. Paul in the New Testament. St. Paul describes the church as a common unity of believers who have all been baptized and have all received the Holy Spirit. "As many of you as were baptized into Christ have clothed yourselves with Christ. There is no longer Jew or Greek, there is no longer slave or free, there is no longer male and female; for all of you are one in Christ Jesus" (Gal 3:27–28).

By reviving St. Paul's notion of the church, the council fathers could reclaim baptism as the center of Christian identity. In a sense, the council "looked backward in order to move forward." Going back to original sources was the way that Vatican II moved ahead in its vision of true Christian community.

In viewing the church as a communion, St. Paul points to the fundamental unity among all the members. This common unity is a bond shared by all the members, past, present, and future, a spiritual bond that transcends even time and space. The communion of the church is an interdependence of all who have ever belonged or will in the future belong to the church. Even death itself does not break or diminish this bond of spiritual communion among the members of the church. The reason for this is that the bond of the communion of the church is the Holy Spirit itself. The "unity of the Spirit in the bond of peace," as St. Paul teaches, is grounded in the "...one hope of your calling, one Lord, one faith, one baptism, one God and Father of all, who is above all and through all and in all" (Eph 4:1, 3–6).

Through baptism, believers enter into the communion of the church and are inserted into this web of relationships. Instead of a power pyramid, the church is more of a circle of relationships empowered by the Holy Spirit. Within this bond of common sharing, there is a diversity of vocations, ministries, and roles in the life of the church. But all are grounded in the deep spiritual unity that has the Spirit of God as its source. St. Paul's insight is that "Now there are varieties of gifts, but the same Spirit; and there are varieties of services, but the same Lord; and there are varieties of activities, but it is the same God who activates all of them in everyone. To each is given the manifestation of the Spirit for the common good" (1 Cor 12:4–7).

The Lay Vocation in the Communion of the Church

The word *vocation* literally means "a calling." Theologically, a vocation is most often described as a calling from God to some state in life. Before the council, the word was usually applied only to the clergy and religious: Those called to the priesthood or religious life "had a vocation," that is, a special calling from God. For the most part, the word was not applied to the laity before Vatican II. The special call seemed to be reserved for priests and vowed religious, whom God called "out of the world" to live a kind of life specially designed to promote holiness. Theirs was a sacred calling to a life popularly considered closer to God than the lives of the laity, who lived "in the world."

By reviving the teaching of the New Testament, the council went back to a more ancient concept of vocation. God calls everyone to relationship with himself. This notion of vocation is really about discipleship in a broad sense. God invites everyone to follow him in an intimate relationship of love with Jesus through the power of the Holy Spirit, and he promises that this relationship of discipleship will enable believers to discover their true selves. In fact, it is only in answering God's call to a life of following him that self-realization can actually take place. Discipleship is a lifelong adventure empowered and illuminated by the Holy Spirit. Jesus himself issues the challenge:

> If any want to become my followers, let them deny themselves and take up their cross and follow me. For

those who want to save their life will lose it, and those who lose their life for my sake, and for the sake of the gospel, will save it. (Mark 8:34–35)

My Father is glorified by this, that you bear much fruit and become my disciples. As the Father has loved me, so I have loved you; abide in my love....You did not choose me but I chose you. And I appointed you to go and bear fruit, fruit that will last.... (John 15:8–9, 16)

In its most basic sense, vocation is the call of God to every person to enter into relationship with him and receive the free gift of salvation. The language of the New Testament speaks of "following Jesus" or "bearing fruit" by remaining in his love. This call of God to relationship is associated with baptism in the New Testament. On the day of Pentecost itself, St. Peter challenged the gathered crowd to answer God's call by repentance, faith, and baptism. "Repent, and be baptized every one of you in the name of Jesus Christ so that your sins may be forgiven; and you will receive the gift of the Holy Spirit. For the promise is for you, for your children, and for all who are far away, everyone whom the Lord our God calls to him" (Acts 2:38–39).

According to this New Testament teaching, every believer has a vocation. St. Peter affirms that this promise of God is for everyone. As the history of the church unfolded, however, the concept of vocation took on another meaning. This secondary meaning of vocation was one's state in life. Vocation became equated with a permanent state in life that was characterized by ordination to holy orders or, in the case of men and women religious, by taking vows. This secondary meaning of vocation was defined by a lifestyle that was "apart from the world." Men and women who "had a vocation" left their families and friends to enter into new communities with others who shared their vocational call. These permanent states of life required years of spiritual formation and academic training. Other things that distinguished these members of the church from others were distinctive dress, housing, and daily schedules that included Mass, prayer in common, and other forms of devotional life.

Up until the 1960s, this secondary meaning of vocation was uppermost in the popular mentality of most Catholics. There were those who were considered to be engaged in an intense Christian lifestyle, and those who were not. The laity were erroneously regarded as not "having a vocation" in the sense of a state of life that was specifically directed toward holiness or some special form of Christian service. While a permanent Christian lifestyle, marriage was not held in very high esteem. Before the council, it was difficult even to find an explanation of the vocation of marriage that did not consider it inferior to or "less holy" than priesthood or religious life. Happily, the teaching of the Second Vatican Council corrected this imbalance.

Vocation as a state of life is a specific context in which a believer lives out the call to discipleship that comes in baptism. Every believer is called to follow Jesus and to "bear fruit" by remaining in his love. Practically speaking, this life of discipleship is lived out in a specific state of life. Baptism comes first, and then the various states of life in the church are ways to live out this basic baptismal call. In this view, marriage takes on an equal dignity with priesthood and religious life. The renewed theology from the council stressed that every believer has a vocation, and the diversity of vocations (states of life) is the work of the Holy Spirit flowing, first of all, from baptism.

Each member of the Body of Christ has a dignity and importance for the whole. According to St. Paul, "...all the members of the body, though many, are one body, so it is with Christ. For in the one Spirit we were all baptized into one body—Jews or Greeks, slaves or free—and we were all made to drink of one Spirit" (1 Cor 12:12–13). There are no second-class citizens in the Body of Christ because baptism is the great equalizer. From baptism flows the secondary meaning of vocation or states in life.

St. Paul speaks of many parts, but one Body. Each baptized believer becomes a member of the one Body. And each part, in turn, has a different role to play. The states of life in the church show this truth of unity in the Body of Christ. When the council spoke of states of life it was in order to show how each of them were ways of living out the Christian call that comes from baptism. The commitments of priesthood, religious life, and the laity are different patterns of the Christian life that are all directed toward holiness and the living out of God's will. This renewed approach to vocation demonstrates the beauty of the diversity of vocations in the communion of the church. While those in holy orders can be involved in secular activities and even in secular profession, they are expressly ordained to the sacred ministry, while those in religious life witness to the necessity of the beatitudes in transforming the world and offering it to God. "But the laity, by their very vocation, seek the kingdom of God by engaging in temporal affairs and by ordering them according to the plan of God" (LG 31).

By emphasizing the teaching of St. Paul and by restoring baptism to its rightful place in the center, Vatican II described the laity and their place in the communion of the church in a much more positive light. Laypeople, incorporated into Christ through baptism, share in the priestly, prophetic, and kingly offices of Christ, and to the best of their ability they carry on the mission of the whole Christian people in the church and in the world (LG 31).

Living Out One's Baptism

If baptism is the fundamental reality for all the states of life in the church, then what effects of baptism bear upon the daily life of the believer? What does the sacrament of baptism provide for the living out of the call to discipleship? As seen above, the vocation of the baptized is the normal, fundamental Christian vocation. Therefore, baptism must be a living reality. It should not be thought of as a past event that usually happens in infancy and has no effect on the daily life of believers. Instead, the whole of the Christian life is a living out of this profound mystery of baptism.

Baptism is a mystery because it is a true sharing in the life of Christ and the means by which the world can be transformed. At a very basic level, the mission of the church is nothing other than the living out of the mystery of baptism in word and deed to bring about the transformation of the world for the sake of Christ. The "energy source" for this mission is the power of the Holy Spirit—the Spirit of God is present in baptism and empowers the lifelong Christian journey of faith. The presence of the Holy Spirit heals, strengthens, and directs the life of one who is living out this mystery, a mystery that is revealed in the very ordinary events of daily life. Rather than a past event, baptism is a reality that bears upon the daily routines and mundane realities of every member of the church.

The theology of baptism is very rich. The New Testament itself offers several powerful images of baptism, and the symbolism of this mystery is quite deep. The three basic aspects of this mystery are regeneration, unification, and anointing. Baptism was the defining event in the lives of the very first Christians since it was a public sign of their desire to commit to the Christian faith. On the day of Pentecost, the beginning of the church itself, three thousand persons accepted the Gospel message and were baptized. "So those who welcomed his message were baptized, and that day about three thousand persons were added" (Acts 2:41).

THE REGENERATION OF BAPTISM

The *regeneration of baptism* refers to the experience of being born anew spiritually. Jesus tells Nicodemus that "no one can see the kingdom of God without being born from above" (John 3:3, 5, 7). Being born "from above" or born again means a spiritual rebirth through the waters of baptism and the power of the Holy Spirit. The one who is baptized becomes a new creation. "So if anyone is in Christ, there is a new creation: everything old has passed away; see, everything has become new!" (2 Cor 5:17). The cleansing waters of baptism bring an end to the power of sin and death and the beginning of a new life in Christ. Baptismal regeneration is about a radical newness, and this new life is one that is lived for God, in Christ, through the power of the Holy Spirit.

> Blessed be the God and Father of our Lord Jesus Christ! By his great mercy he has given us a new birth into a living hope through the resurrection of Jesus Christ from the dead, and into an inheritance that is imperishable, undefiled, and unfading, kept in heaven for you, who are being protected by the power of God through faith for a salvation ready to be revealed in the last time. (1 Pet 1:3–5)

This new birth gives a new identity that the New Testament describes as adoption. The baptized are adopted as sons and daughters of God the Father. No longer alienated from God through sin, now the believer is spiritually adopted into an intimate relationship with God. The meaning and implications of this new identity as members of God's own family take a lifetime to unfold. The true identity of the baptized must be realized in daily life, relationships, and activities. Once this basic reality of divine adoption is grasped, then the power of the Holy Spirit can inform and shape the life of the believer in big and small ways.

Through baptism, God has sent the Holy Spirit to dwell in the hearts of believers and to teach them how to live as children of God. "And because you are children, God has sent the Spirit of his Son into our hearts, crying, 'Abba! Father!' " (Gal 4:6). This adoption, this spirit of sonship, is the spiritual power for daily living.

> For all who are led by the Spirit of God are children of God. For you did not receive a spirit of slavery to fall back into fear, but you have received a spirit of adoption. When we cry, "Abba! Father!" it is that very Spirit bearing witness with our spirit that we are children of God. (Rom 8:14–16)

THE UNIFICATION OF BAPTISM

In addition to regeneration and adoption, baptism also unites believers with Christ and with one another. The baptized are incorporated into Christ's body in a mystical way and are profoundly united with other members of the church. Baptism plunges one into the communion of the church by the unifying bond of the Holy Spirit. Thus the Christian life is not a private enterprise or an individualistic affair, but a life lived in community. "For as in one body we have many members, and not all the members have the same function, so we, who are many, are one body in Christ, and individually we are members one of another" (Rom 12:4–5).

The mystical incorporation of believers into this unity is described as an entrance into the death and resurrection of Jesus. Entrance into the waters of baptism is an entrance into Christ's death. Coming up out of the waters is an entrance into his resurrection. And this is not merely an external sign or symbol. Rather, on a deep mystical level, the one who is baptized is actually entering into this reality of Christ's dying and rising. Being plunged into the water is a true death to sin and to the former way of life. Arising from the waters is a literal entrance into the gift of eternal life and a new creation. St. Paul in his Letter to the Romans puts it this way:

> Do you not know that all of us who have been baptized into Christ Jesus were baptized into his death? Therefore we have been buried with him by baptism into death, so that, just as Christ was raised from the dead by the glory of the Father, so we too might walk in newness of life. For if we have been united with him in a death like his, we will certainly be united with him in a resurrection like his. (Rom 6:3–5)

The reality of Christ's death and resurrection is known as the "paschal mystery." This phrase refers to the mystery of Christ's triumph over sin and death on Good Friday and his entrance into glorified, resurrected life on Easter Sunday. This cycle of dying and rising is the saving mystery into which one is incorporated through baptism. Living out the mystery of baptism is not just being freed from the powers of sin and death; it also means a whole new kind of life which is a life in relationship with God and other members of the church. This new life is a unifying life, unifying believers with one another and with the Father, Son, and Holy Spirit.

> Thus by baptism men are plunged into the paschal mystery of Christ: they die with Him, are buried with Him, and rise with Him they receive the spirit of adoption as sons "in which we cry: Abba, Father" (Rom 8:15), and thus become true adorers whom the Father seeks. (SC 6)

Living out the mystery of baptism means allowing the pattern of the paschal mystery to become the pattern of one's life. The dying and rising cycle is the growth pattern in the life of any believer. It means a daily decision to say no to sin and yes to God.

The "dying" is a dying to selfishness and self will. And the "rising" is faithful obedience to God's will and allowing the power of the Holy Spirit to set the course for life and action. "So you also must consider yourselves dead to sin and alive to God in Christ Jesus" (Rom 6:11).

Living the paschal mystery is the process of transformation in the Christian life. It is a slow transformation as one dies to sin and to anything else that would distract from the focus of following Jesus. This, of course, includes hard choices that sometimes bring suffering. But dying to self produces spiritual fruit and the new life of the resurrection that can be also be experienced in daily life. The resurrected life of the paschal mystery means deeper meaning, love, and a deeper sense of community. Because of incorporation into the Body of Christ, one does not live this challenging life of discipleship in isolation. The vital union of believers with God and with one another is the source of its life. This is true because the Holy Spirit is the bond that forms the communion of the church.

THE ANOINTING OF BAPTISM

The sacrament of baptism is also an anointing. The dove that descended upon Jesus at his own baptism is a symbol of his anointing by the Holy Spirit (Mark 1:9–11). The titles "Christ" and "Messiah" mean the "anointed one." Jesus is the anointed one, the Messiah, sent by the Father to bring the kingdom of God in its fullness. Jesus claims this anointing when he declares that he has been sent by the Father to usher in the salvation promised by the prophets in the Old Testament. Reading the scroll from the prophet Isaiah in the synagogue, Jesus says:

> The Spirit of the Lord is upon me, because he has anointed me to bring good news to the poor. He has sent me to proclaim release to the captives and recovery of sight to the blind, to let the oppressed go free, to proclaim the year of the Lord's favor....Today this scripture has been fulfilled in your hearing. (Luke 4:18–21)

The Holy Spirit was the power behind the earthly ministry of Jesus. The Spirit led Jesus into the wilderness immediately after his baptism and strengthened him to resist the temptations of the devil while in the wilderness for forty days, as he was spiritually prepared for his public ministry (Mark 1, Luke 4, Matthew 4). Once the public ministry began, it was the Holy Spirit that empowered the preaching and teaching of Jesus. His miracles, exorcisms, and forgiveness of sins were all evidence of the power of the Spirit to overcome the powers of evil, sin, and death. Jesus, the anointed one, fulfilled the prophecies of the Old Testament, ushered in the kingdom of God by his words and deeds, and revealed the love of God through the dynamism of the Holy Spirit.

After his death and resurrection, Jesus communicated the Holy Spirit to his apostles as he established the church. Jesus "breathed on them and said to them, 'Receive the Holy Spirit' " (John 20:19–23). The Holy Spirit would equip the apostles for carrying out the mission of Jesus after the ascension. Jesus promised this empowerment before he returned to the Father's right hand in heaven. At the ascension, he exhorted them to remain in Jerusalem, where they would receive power from God. This promise of Jesus was fulfilled at Pentecost. The Holy Spirit's power came upon them in a very dynamic way to enable them to continue the mission of Jesus in the world (Acts of the Apostles 1—2) Anointed by the Holy Spirit, the apostles and early Christians boldly proclaimed the resurrection of Jesus and accomplished many signs and wonders to show the healing power of the kingdom of God.

In his theology of baptism, St. Paul explains that the anointing of the Holy Spirit makes believers into "temples of the Holy Spirit." This image comes from the actual Jewish temple in Jerusalem. The ancient Jews believed that God dwelt with the ark of the covenant, the sacred object that contained the tablets of the Law, brought down from Mount Sinai by Moses himself. In the days of ancient Israel, the ark of the covenant was kept in the innermost sanctuary of the temple and not accessible to the ordinary Jewish believer. Only the high priest could enter the sanctuary, known as the "holy of holies." It was believed that God's Spirit dwelt with the ark of the covenant, making it God's mercy seat or throne. The temple, then, housed the Spirit of God in a very powerful and mysterious way.

St. Paul uses this imagery to describe baptized believers as "temples." "Do you not know that you are God's temple and that God's Spirit dwells in you? For God's temple is holy, and you are that temple" (1 Cor 3:16–17). Baptism brings about an anointing of the Holy Spirit so that each believer is like a walking temple, a movable tabernacle. The indwelling of the Holy Spirit empowers the believer to live the Christian life of daily discipleship. The dynamism of the indwelling Holy Spirit allows the believer to grow in holiness and thereby bring about the kingdom in big and small ways in the midst of daily life.

The anointing of the Holy Spirit forms the members of the church, collectively, into a spiritual temple: "...like living stones, let yourselves be built into a spiritual house..." (1 Pet 2:5). The whole church, then, is like a living temple, with the Holy Spirit dwelling in the heart of each member. The indwelling of the Holy Spirit is the animating life principle of the church and allows the church to live the message and mission of Christ in the world. The life of the church grows and deepens in relation to how each member of the church yields to this power of the Holy Spirit. "In him the whole structure is joined together and grows into a holy temple in the Lord; in whom you also are built together spiritually into a dwelling place for God" (Eph 2:21–22).

As this review of New Testament theology has demonstrated, the theology of baptism is rich and complex. The three basic aspects of regeneration, unification, and anointing all highlight the power of the Holy Spirit that infuses every vocation in the life of the church. Baptism is the foundation for identity and mission for each member of the church, as the council made clear. Putting baptism back into the center helped to rebalance the theology of the church and inspire the lay faithful to understand the dignity of their vocation. The old "pay, pray, and obey" model of the unequal society can no longer be considered valid, and the Second Vatican Council's emphasis on baptism ensures that the laity will never be considered second-class citizens again.

The Secular Character of the Laity

The council fathers' focus on baptism reveals their interest in motivating the laity to live their faith, to claim their baptismal identity in daily life. Since baptism is the source of Christian existence and life, the meaning of baptism reveals the very meaning of the Christian life. And this New Testament meaning provides the very motivation for living out the Christian faith in daily life. The newness of baptism, the bond of relationships with other believers and God, and the anointing of the Holy Spirit all combine to be the dynamism for ongoing conversion. This seems to be the practical focus of the council's teaching.

This focus might be summed up in the exhortation: "Become what you are." There is an urgent call in the teaching of Vatican II for each member of the church to reclaim his or her baptism so that it actually makes a practical difference in their relationships, activities, and pursuits. The encouragement and motivation offered to laypeople in particular is an insistence on uniting identity with action, or the paschal mystery with real life. Unfortunately, in the unequal society or power pyramid models of the church there was usually a disconnect in the understanding of the baptismal identity of the laity and their call to daily discipleship and holiness. Since the laity were considered "worldly" and their daily lives "profane," it was difficult to see how their life in the world could be connected to their Christian existence.

In contrast, Vatican II's theology of baptism embraced the ordinariness of the lay life as an opportunity for spiritual growth and purpose. The mundane lives of laypersons, when empowered by the mystery of baptism, become the very occasion of God's call to transformation. Once considered a "concession to human weakness," the lay vocation became viewed as an opportunity to seek the kingdom of God. Because of the centrality of baptism, the lay vocation is equal in dignity and importance to the vocations of the clergy and religious.

In its attempt to show the practicality of baptism for ordinary life, the council developed the phrase *secular character*. This phrase was meant to affirm the reality that the lay life, lived in the midst of the world, is an opportunity to seek the kingdom of God.

Secular character is a manner of life that distinguishes laypeople. The council states that the laity, "by their very vocation, seek the kingdom of God by engaging in temporal affairs and by ordering them according to the plan of God" (LG 31). But this distinctiveness does not somehow separate the laity from clergy and religious in the common call to holiness. Instead, secular character should be considered from within an understanding of the communion of all the members of the church.

In order to appreciate the position of the laity in the communion of the church in light of their secular character, it is necessary to understand that the whole church has a secular dimension. God's plan of salvation and the ongoing process of the redemption of the world include the entire People of God. As the New Testament makes clear, all Christians live in the world, even if they do not take on the values of the world.

In John's gospel, "the world" is often identified with all that is opposed to the teachings of Jesus and the reality of the kingdom of God. Being "worldly" in John's gospel means being in opposition to Jesus, who is the true light of the world. Therefore, Jesus says that his followers live *in* the world but they are not *of* the world. "They do not belong to the world, just as I do not belong to the world" (John 17:16). And yet, Jesus sends his followers into the world to spread his kingdom and truth. Jesus prays to his Father: "As you have sent me into the world, so I have sent them into the world. And for their sakes I sanctify myself, so that they also may be sanctified in truth" (John 17:17–19).

Christians are sent into the world on a mission to continue the redeeming work of Christ. In this way, the ongoing redemption of the world is accomplished through the church, the communion of the baptized. Every believer shares in this mission and responsibility. All members of the church are sent into the world for the salvation of the whole human race and the renewal of the whole temporal order. This is what is meant by saying that the church has a secular dimension inherent to its nature and mission. It is in the very nature of the church to be sent on mission and renew the world with the power of the Holy Spirit received in baptism. Christ's redemptive work is essentially concerned with human salvation and yet also includes the renewal of the entire temporal order. Thus the mission of the Church is not only to proclaim the message and grace of Christ but also "to penetrate and perfect the temporal order with the spirit of the Gospel" (AA 5).

The whole church has a secular dimension and all the baptized share in it, although in different ways. The laity share in the secular dimension in a distinctive way, as do clergy and religious men and women. Indeed, each of these states of life is a proper and particular way of sharing in the secular dimension of the whole church. In highlighting the secular character of the laity, the council stressed that the lay faithful live in the world, in the ordinary circumstances of everyday life, and engage in the secular professions and occupations. "They are called there by God that by exercising their proper function and led by the spirit of the Gospel they may work for the sanctification of the world from within as a leaven" (LG 31).

The conciliar teaching on secular character demonstrates how seriously the council considered the daily lives of the laity. All the situations of daily life find their deepest meaning in light of the mystery of Christ. The newness of baptism gives a newness to even the most ordinary situations and activities. This is because it is in the particular situation of the laity in the world that God reveals his plan and communicates to them their particular way of "seeking the kingdom of God by engaging in temporal affairs and by ordering them according to the plan of God" (LG 31).

By highlighting the notion of secular character, the council affirmed the importance of the temporal activities of the laity. Mundane activities and pursuits are the raw materials for living out the mystery of baptism. Each day, laypeople have an opportunity to identify their lives with the redeeming mystery of Christ and the reality of the kingdom of God. The secular character of the laity means that their daily concerns can find deep meaning and fulfillment in the radical newness of baptism, which is their Christian experience. The council stressed the God-given intrinsic value of everything that comprises the secular order, including "the good things of life and the prosperity of the family, culture, economic matters, the arts and professions, the laws of the political community, international relations, and other matters of this kind." All these things have an intrinsic value established by God. "God saw that all He had made was very good" (Gen 1:31; see AA 7).

The secular character of the laity is not just about where the laity live—in the world. It is, in a deeper sense, about how and why laypersons live out their ordinary lives in awareness of their baptismal identity. That is, the secular character is not just a sociological aspect of the vocation of the laity but a theological truth of their call by God to share in the redeeming work of Christ through the power of the Holy Spirit. Baptism gives the laity a share in the creating and redeeming work of God, and they participate in realizing the kingdom of God through their secular character. The position or vocation of laity in the church becomes defined by the new reality of the Christian life and distinguished by their secular character.

The secular character of laypersons—their presence and activity in the world—is not something that is merely incidental but, as the council observes, is central to their vocation. The world is the environment and the means by which the lay faithful live out their baptismal call. The emphasis on the secular character of the laity cannot be construed, however, to make a hard and fast dichotomy between the mission of the laity and that of the clergy and men and women religious. Certainly there are distinctions within the communion of the church; but this does not mean that the world is the domain of the laity while the church is the sole responsibility of the clergy and religious.

The necessary promotion of the laity's mission in the world cannot mean that the church's inner life should be thought of as the exclusive preserve of the clergy and religious and the world the only place for the laity. This theologically incorrect "church vs. world" position has no basis in the teachings of the council and would lead to a highly clericalized church and a laity with little or no sense of their own vocation and a feeling of being second-class citizens. A two-sphere approach to mission would take the lay faithful back to the old "pay, pray, and obey" model of the inner life of the church. For this reason the council teaches that the *entire* church has an authentic secular dimension in which all members share, but in different ways.

1987 Synod on the Laity

In 1984, Pope John Paul II announced that the theme of the next synod of bishops would be the vocation and mission of the laity. That the bishops of the church would consider the vocation and mission of the laity more than twenty years after Vatican II was significant. In choosing to have the laity as the subject of reflection and discussion at the 1987 synod, Pope John Paul II affirmed the central importance of the theology of the laity in the years following Vatican II, a theology that emphasized their full membership in the church and their responsibility for its mission. The time was ripe for evaluating how effectively this renewed theology was being applied around the world since the council.

The aim of the 1987 synod was to follow paths laid out by the Second Vatican Council in treating the topic of the vocation and mission of the laity. Indeed, the theology of the council was the constant reference point for the bishops' discussions and deliberations. The bishops wanted to spell out concretely how the council's theology of the laity could be translated into practice. In so doing, they desired to promote a deeper awareness, among all the members of the church, of the gift and responsibility they share in the communion and mission of the church.

At the end of the 1987 synod, the bishops asked that a conclusive document be written by the pope himself on the topic of the laity. This document turned out to be the 1988 Post-Synodal Papal Exhortation, *Christifideles Laici*, On the Vocation and Mission of the Lay Faithful in the Church and in the World. Without doubt, this is the most important papal document on the laity since the Second Vatican Council. Its aim is clearly to inspire a competent, generous, and resolute laity to embrace their responsibilities in the church and in the world, calling them to live as salt for the earth and light to the world.

The first chapter of *Christifideles Laici* echoes the council's call to put baptism "back in the center." By beginning with a theology of baptism, Pope John Paul II confirms the truth that the vocation of the laity is not to second-class citizenship in the church.

Incorporation into Christ through faith and Baptism is the source of being a Christian in the mystery of the Church. This mystery constitutes the Christian's most basic features and serves as the basis for all the vocations and dynamism of the Christian life of the lay faithful (John 3:5)....Therefore, only through accepting the richness in mystery that God gives to the Christian in Baptism is it possible to come to a basic description of the lay faithful.[1]

The centrality of baptism receives further emphasis in section 10, which declares that the entire purpose of the lay faithful's existence is "to lead a person to a knowledge of the radical newness of the Christian life that comes from Baptism, the sacrament of faith, so that this knowledge can help that person live the responsibilities which arise from that vocation received from God."

The three aspects of the mystery of baptism discussed above were also part of the pope's teaching. First, baptism regenerates believers in the life of the Son of God by the power of the Holy Spirit (CFL 11).

Second, in a mystical but real way, baptism incorporates believers into Christ and his Body (CFL 12).

Third, baptism is the anointing of the Holy Spirit, who seals each baptized person with an indelible character, filling him or her with the holy presence of God (CFL 13).

Baptismal identity is the foundation for equality and common dignity among all the members of the church. As a result, each lay Christian shares with the ordained and religious a responsibility for the church's mission. Within this common vocation and mission, the laity have a "...manner of life which sets a person apart, without however, bringing about a separation from the ministerial priesthood or from men and women religious...the secular character" (CFL 15).

These passages from the pope's exhortation both confirm the teachings of Vatican II and challenge all the members of the church to implement and live out this profound theology of vocation and mission that flows from baptism. Truly, the days of the unequal society model of the church, with its passive view of the laity and its negative approach to the lay vocation and mission were over.

Conclusion

It is difficult to overestimate the importance of reclaiming the New Testament theology of baptism for the theology of the laity. The Second Vatican Council stressed a positive view of the vocation of the laity that enabled them to realize their dignity and responsibilities in the church. In place of the power pyramid, which presented a passive laity, the council offered the exciting vision of the church as a communion. Within the communion of believers, it is possible to perceive what the laity share with all the other members of the church, as well as the distinctiveness of the laity's vocation and mission.

The distinctive secular character of laypersons does not exclude them from a life of discipleship and holiness, but instead reveals the value of their daily lives as opportunities for Christian growth. The rebirth of baptism provides spiritual newness to their most mundane activities, duties, and experiences. By living out their baptism, the laity share in the creating and redeeming work of God and thereby participate in the realization of the kingdom of God.

Reflection Questions

1. How do you experience the graces of baptism in daily life?

2. Where have you seen most clearly the shifts in the Catholic understanding of vocation and call?

3. In what times and places is the communion of all the vocations in the church most evident?

4. Why is the "secular character" of the lay vocation such a critical component in any theology of the laity?

CHAPTER THREE

The Laity's Call to Holiness

Holiness—Not for a Select Few

The Second Vatican Council's teaching on the universal vocation of all the Christian faithful to holiness was clearly part of the "New Pentecost" envisioned by Pope John XXIII. The Holy Spirit seemed to be prompting the church to rediscover the reality of holiness as found in the New Testament. By offering a fresh appreciation for the mystery of baptism, the council could then explore the richness of holiness that had too often been neglected. All members of the church were challenged to become more aware of their incorporation into Christ through their baptism. A notion of holiness was then formulated that did not take the laity out of the world, but rather made them aware of God's presence in the world and in their own personal experiences.

Traditionally, the average layperson considered holiness in this life to be the almost exclusive domain of clergy and religious. Therefore, anyone who wanted to become a truly holy and dedicated Christian would have to enter religious life, thereby separating oneself from the messiness of the affairs of the world. Of course this was a false idea—but it had a profound effect on how most laypersons understood the Christian life and their own personal relationship with God. Another factor that compounded this situation was that laypersons were usually called simply to "avoid sin" rather than to "be holy." The very phrasing of these moral imperatives was a way of communicating low expectations for lay sanctity. The negative "avoidance of sin" was thought to be more appropriate for the laity than the positive admonition to "be holy."

The notion of holiness proposed by the council is the exact opposite of the invitation to leave this world and to look for union with God elsewhere, which was usually the spiritual advice given to the laity in the past. Unfortunately, the gift of salvation was often presented as something to be enjoyed only in the afterlife. Being saved meant dying and going to heaven. With so much insistence in the past on receiving the "last sacraments" and dying in a state of grace, it is no wonder that some lay men and women were not sufficiently aware of their call to live and grow in grace and holiness in *this* life. Without an emphasis on the spiritual value of daily life, it is nearly impossible to see daily activities, sufferings, joys, and hopes as opportunities to grow in holiness and union with God.

Christ's exhortation to holiness focuses on the here and now, not simply on life after death. There is no state of life or condition that should hinder this growth in holiness. Being a member of the laity is not an obstacle to intimacy with God and the journey of spiritual perfection. Vatican II reiterates this truth: "...all the faithful, whatever their condition or state, are called by the Lord, each in his own way, to that perfect holiness whereby the Father Himself is perfect" (LG 11).

Through the reclamation of the New Testament theology of baptism, the Second Vatican Council opened the way for a fresh appreciation of the call to all members of the church to grow in grace and charity to Christian maturity through a conscious experience of union with God in daily life.

Old Testament Teaching on Holiness

Christian teaching on holiness is based upon the Jewish understanding of holiness as found in the Old Testament and is very similar to the exhortations of Moses and the Prophets. For example, in Leviticus 11 the ancient Hebrews are urged to be holy since God himself is holy. Holiness is one of the characteristics of God, and in their relationship with God, the Hebrews are called to be holy as well.

> For I am the LORD your God; sanctify yourselves therefore, and be holy, for I am holy....For I am the LORD who

brought you up from the land of Egypt, to be your God;
you shall be holy, for I am holy. (Lev 11:44–45)

This brief passage from Leviticus contains several important
elements of the Old Testament teaching on holiness. First, it
mentions God's action of salvation. God acted to save the Hebrew
people from slavery in Egypt in the Exodus. He accomplished the
mighty deeds of their deliverance; they themselves did nothing to
earn or merit God's actions to save them. His salvation is freely
given. Second, the relationship that this action forged is highlighted. God has become their Lord and God as a result of his own
initiative in bringing them out of Egypt. He did these awesome
deeds so that he might be their God and they might be his people.

Next, this passage presents holiness as a characteristic of
God himself. Holiness is part of the divine nature. God affirms
twice in this short passage that his holiness is an important part
of his identity. Finally, the people are called to holiness. God
exhorts them to be holy and keep themselves holy. And this call
cannot be understood apart from their relationship with God.
Holiness is something that flows from God's identity into his saving deeds and permeates their relationship with him.

Theologically speaking, Leviticus 11 presents the covenant
between God and the ancient Hebrews. The covenant is a relationship or a solemn agreement that God entered into with his people
in the context of the Exodus events. This brief passage alludes to all
these mighty deeds—the parting of the Red Sea, the giving of the
Ten Commandments, the gift of the Promised Land. As a result of
the Exodus, Moses and the people pledged themselves to a covenantal relationship in which they would forsake all false gods and serve
and worship God alone. This exclusive relationship brought with it
demands and moral claims on the lives of each member of the community. Holiness is one of the ways these demands are described.

HOLINESS AS GIFT AND CHALLENGE

Interestingly, this Old Testament teaching on holiness has
two dimensions. First, holiness is both a gift from God and a challenge to be lived out in daily life. In his action of saving the people

and bringing them into relationship with him, God bestows holiness upon them. The people become holy simply because God has saved them. They did not earn or merit this holiness; it comes as a result of their covenantal relationship with God. In his actions of deliverance, God communicates his own holiness to them and they become sharers in this aspect of divine life, God's own life. This participation or sharing in God's own holiness is a sheer gift from the God who brought them up out of Egypt.

The second dimension of holiness is how the ancient Hebrews are to live out this relationship with God in a practical way. Their exclusive covenant with God affords them a deep participation in his own divine life. Once this gift of holiness is received, they must live it out in daily life—they must "keep themselves holy," as Leviticus 11 states. The way they conduct themselves as individuals and as a community is to be characterized by holiness. This challenge to be holy is a call to make the covenant with God absolutely central in their lives so that it shapes how they live. They are to enflesh and make practical their participation in God's own holiness.

These two aspects or dimensions of holiness might be described as *objective* and *subjective*. Objectively speaking, God is holy. He is the source of all holiness. The awesome majesty and transcendent splendor of his holiness is unique since it is part of God's inner divine life and nature. God himself refers to this objective dimension of holiness many times in the Old Testament when he simply says, "I am holy," as stated in Leviticus. It is this objective holiness of God that was revealed in the Exodus events. At the parting of the Red Sea, in fact, the Hebrews acclaim this holiness: "Who is like you, O Lord, among the gods? Who is like you, majestic in holiness, awesome in splendor, doing wonders?" (Ex 15:11).

This objective holiness of God is what God freely shares with the ancient Hebrews in the covenantal relationship. By sharing in God's objective holiness, the community takes on the identity of being a holy people. This reality does not depend on the actions or merits of the people themselves, but is rooted in God's action of salvation.

The second dimension of holiness is the subjective one. Once the people are redeemed and become sharers in God's objective holiness, then the challenge is issued to live out this new identity.

47

"You shall be holy, for I the Lord your God am holy" (Lev 19:2). Indeed, the call to subjective holiness means simply to live in the covenant relationship with God day in and day out. Being holy is not a matter of trying to achieve a certain moral status; rather, it is to live out the relationship that has already been freely given by God in his love and mercy. Because the people share in God's objective holiness, they must live in a certain way. Their subjective call to live a holy life is really a way of expressing gratitude to the God who saved them and made them his own people. Responding to the demands and responssibilities of their covenant with God is their subjective challenge of holiness. "Indeed, the whole earth is mine, but you shall be for me a priestly kingdom and a holy nation" (Exod 19:5–6).

PROPHETIC TRADITIONS

The prophets of the Old Testament also present this twofold teaching on holiness, emphasizing the identity of Israel as God's holy nation because of his action in saving them and making them his own. They also spend much of their prophetic ministry exhorting the people not to forsake this identity. While affirming their unique relationship with God among all of the nations, the prophets urge the Israelites to a manner of life that fulfills the subjective call to holiness as a public witness of this relationship. Israel, as a nation, should witness to their covenant with God by living in a way that sets them apart from the other nations who do not know God.

Isaiah is one example of an Old Testament prophet who reminded the people of Israel of their covenant with God as well as their responsibility to live it out. When God calls Isaiah to be a prophet, it is in the context of a vision of his holiness. Isaiah is given a glimpse of God's objective holiness and it changes him forever. God's holiness is an awesome thing, and Isaiah has an experience of it as he is praying in the temple. In a mystical vision, Isaiah sees God's throne and the worship of the angels who acclaim him as holy.

I saw the Lord sitting on a throne, high and lofty....Seraphs were in attendance above him; each had six wings....And one called to another and said: "Holy, holy, holy is the LORD of hosts; the whole earth is full of his glory." (Isa 6:1–3)

This glimpse of God's objective holiness marks Isaiah as a prophet and deeply influences his future prophetic messages. The words and prophecies of Isaiah focus on this so much that he can rightly be called the "prophet of holiness." According to Isaiah's teaching, Israel is holy because of what God has done for them in his act of saving them. "Whoever is left in Zion and remains in Jerusalem will be called holy, everyone who has been recorded for life in Jerusalem" (Isa 4:3). As a result of God's redeeming action, Israel shares in the objective holiness of God. "Say to daughter Zion, 'See, your salvation comes; his reward is with him, and his recompense before him.' They shall be called, 'The Holy People, The Redeemed of the Lord' " (Isa 62:11–12).

Isaiah constantly emphasizes that Israel is obliged to make this holiness manifest in its life as a nation. He explicitly links its subjective call to holiness with justice. God, the "holy one of Israel," demands a people who are just and righteous. "But the Lord of hosts is exalted by justice, and the Holy God shows himself holy by righteousness" (Isa 5:16). The prophet cries out against injustice because oppression of the poor, the widow, and the orphan—the most vulnerable in society—is an affront to God's holiness. Isaiah connects holiness to justice in very concrete ways.

Ah, you who make iniquitous decrees, who write oppressive statutes, to turn aside the needy from justice and to rob the poor of my people of their right, that widows may be your spoil, and that you may make the orphans your prey! What will you do on the day of punishment, in the calamity that will come from far away? (Isa 10:1–3)

Isaiah's prophecies make it clear that holiness is both a gift and a challenge, an unmerited privilege as well as a call to righteousness.

In summary, the Old Testament has a rich theology of holiness. This brief analysis of passages from Leviticus and Isaiah gives at least a taste of this richness. The experience of the ancient

Hebrews in the deliverance of the Exodus events and the history of their life as the nation of Israel reveals the wonder of holiness. It is this Jewish understanding of holiness that forms the basis for the Christian theology of holiness in the New Testament.

New Testament Teaching on Holiness

The call to holiness in the New Testament is issued by Jesus himself. Jesus is the holy one of God (John 6:69). The son of Mary is the holy Son of God (Luke 1:35), and he calls his followers to holiness of life. Grounded in the rich Jewish notion of holiness, Jesus deepens and expands it by making it available to all believers, not just to a select few. It is not just the "religious professionals" who are called to a higher righteousness; everyone must answer this call. "For I tell you, unless your righteousness exceeds that of the scribes and Pharisees, you will never enter the kingdom of heaven....Be perfect, therefore, as your heavenly Father is perfect" (Matt 5:20, 48; see also LG 40).

The New Testament notion of holiness contains the same four basic elements as the Old Testament. First, God's own action of salvation is central. But instead of focusing on the Exodus events, the New Testament is centered on the death and resurrection of Jesus. His self-gift on the cross and his rising on the third day bring about salvation available to all who believe. By his Easter victory, Jesus accomplishes the Father's plan to bring forgiveness, healing, and new life. God's action of salvation is the reconciliation of the whole world to himself through the dying and rising of Jesus. "But God proves his love for us in that while we still were sinners Christ died for us" (Rom 5:8).

GOD'S ACTION OF SALVATION

This action of salvation is a free gift. There was nothing the human race could do to earn or merit this gift. The faithful are "justified in the Lord Jesus, because in the baptism of faith they truly become sons of God and sharers in the divine nature" (LG 40). Christians are "sanctified" or made holy by God's action and not their own accomplishments. God, in his love and mercy, sent

Jesus to reveal the kingdom of God and to accomplish the redemption of the whole world.

> But God, who is rich in mercy, out of the great love with which he loved us even when we were dead through our trespasses, made us alive together with Christ....For by grace you have been saved through faith, and this is not your own doing; it is the gift of God—not the result of works, so that no one may boast. (Eph 2:4–9)

By offering himself on the cross, Jesus made holiness possible for all who believe. Much like the Old Testament theology, holiness is a result of God's action in saving his people. "Christ loved the church and gave himself up for her, in order to make her holy by cleansing her with the washing of water by the word, so as to present the church to himself in splendor, without a spot or wrinkle or anything of the kind—yes, so that she may be holy and without blemish" (Eph 5:25–27).

THE NEW COVENANTAL COMMUNITY

The second element in the notion of holiness is that God's act of redemption forms a new community. Borrowing the language of Exodus, the New Testament recounts how God's act of mercy in Jesus brings about a people he claims for his own.

> But you are a chosen race, a royal priesthood, a holy nation, God's own people....Once you were not a people, but now you are God's people; once you had not received mercy, but now you have received mercy. (1 Pet 2:9–10)

This second element, then, is the relationship forged by God's action of salvation. No longer just restricted to the Jewish community, the New Testament presents a theology of the "new covenant" between God and anyone who believes. This new solemn agreement or covenant is sealed not with animal's blood as in the Exodus story, but rather with Jesus' own blood. "...he entered once for all into the Holy Place, not with the blood of goats and calves, but with his own blood, thus obtaining eternal redemption....For this reason he is the mediator of a new covenant, so that those who are called may receive the promised eternal inheritance" (Heb 9:12, 15).

Jesus himself uses covenantal language to describe the meaning of his death. At the Last Supper, he uses the cup of wine as a way to explain the new relationship with God that will be possible through his cross. "This cup that is poured out for you is the new covenant in my blood" (Luke 22:20). Christians, therefore, form the new covenantal community in their relationship with God and one another, through Jesus, in the power of the Holy Spirit. This bond or relationship of the new covenant brings with it demands and moral claims on the lives of each member of the church. And holiness is one of the ways in which these demands are described.

GOD AS THE SOURCE OF ALL HOLINESS

The third aspect of the New Testament theology of holiness also reflects the Old Testament teaching. Holiness is a characteristic of God himself. "...Christ, the Son of God, who with the Father and the Spirit is praised as 'uniquely holy'..." (LG 39). In fact, the New Testament directly borrows the teaching from Leviticus. "...as he who called you is holy, be holy yourselves in all your conduct; for it is written, 'You shall be holy, for I am holy' " (1 Pet 1:15–16).

This quotation from 1 Peter highlights both the objective and subjective dimensions of holiness explained above. Objectively speaking, God is holy and is the source of all holiness. The First Letter of Peter follows the prophet Isaiah in presenting holiness as part of the divine nature. This objective holiness is communicated to Christians in their experience of baptism. Baptism plunges one into the death and resurrection of Jesus, the paschal mystery, and this brings the free gift of salvation and therefore a sharing in God's own objective holiness. Baptized Christians participate in the very life of God himself.

It is the presence of the Holy Spirit, the objective holiness of God, that makes the church holy. The indwelling of the Holy Spirit in the hearts of believers is a deep participation in God's objective holiness. "God's love has been poured into our hearts through the Holy Spirit that has been given to us" (Rom 5:5). Each Christian is a kind of building block in the holy temple that is God's church.

And the indwelling of the Holy Spirit in this temple makes the church holy. "In him the whole structure is joined together and grows into a holy temple in the Lord; in whom you also are built together spiritually into a dwelling place for God" (Eph 2:21–22).

HOLINESS IN ORDINARY LIFE

Finally, baptized believers are challenged to live out this holiness subjectively in their daily lives and conduct. The imperative of 1 Peter to "be holy" is a call to enflesh the new life given to them in the rebirth of baptism. Although similar in language to the call to holiness from Leviticus, what is distinctive about the New Testament call to holiness is the theology of the Holy Spirit. The Holy Spirit comes to dwell in the hearts of believers through baptism and therefore gives them a share in God's objective holiness. "Do you not know that your body is a temple of the Holy Spirit within you, which you have from God, and that you are not your own? For you were bought with a price; therefore glorify God in your body" (1 Cor 6:19–20).

The Holy Spirit of God not only dwells within believers, but it also empowers them to answer the call to holiness in daily life. The power of the Holy Spirit energizes and enables Christians to live a subjectively holy life. It is a matter not of human striving but of openness to the power of the Spirit: "...the Spirit helps us in our weakness" (Rom 8:26). Answering the call to holiness is a matter of being led by the Spirit of God and yielding to its promptings in the midst of daily life. St. Paul points out that "all who are led by the Spirit of God are children of God" (Rom 8:14) and warns the faithful to live "as becomes saints" (see LG 40).

The subjective call to holiness in the New Testament is really an invitation to members of the church to allow the Holy Spirit to lead them in every aspect of their conduct. "If we live by the Spirit, let us also be guided by the Spirit" (Gal 5:25). The invitation is to allow the presence of God within to direct one's thoughts and actions in a growth toward Christian maturity. The life of holiness is all about this ongoing transformation. And without it, there really is no discernable Christian life. "Pursue the holiness without which no one will see the Lord" (Heb 12:14).

The evidence that one is growing in the Christian life and being led by the Spirit is the presence of the fruits of the Holy Spirit. As a tree is known by its fruits, so a life of Christian holiness is known by the presence of these virtues (see LG 39). St. Paul gives a partial listing of these fruits of grace. "The fruit of the Spirit is love, joy, peace, patience, kindness, generosity, faithfulness, gentleness, and self-control" (Gal 5:22–23). The imagery of fruits being produced implies the process of organic growth. Holiness is not something static; it is a constant evolution. Bearing fruit is a maturation process that slowly unfolds.

Jesus himself uses this agricultural metaphor of bearing fruit. Likening believers to branches on a vine, Jesus teaches that he is the main stem of this vine. Through baptism, Christians are grafted on to this vine and receive their spiritual nutrition from its life. Just as the life of a vine feeds the branches, so too, the life of Jesus gives strength and sustenance to anyone living in relationship with him. Branches depend on a vine and Christians depend on Jesus for their spiritual lifeblood. By being connected to Jesus, the branches can bear fruit. Participation in the divine life yields a fruitfulness that can also be called holiness. Objectively speaking, Christians are holy simply because they have become branches by being grafted on to Jesus, the vine. And subjectively they are then called to allow his life to flow through them and bear spiritual fruit manifested in a life of holiness. In John's gospel, Jesus enjoins his believers:

> Abide in me as I abide in you. Just as the branch cannot bear fruit by itself unless it abides in the vine, neither can you unless you abide in me. I am the vine, you are the branches. Those who abide in me and I in them bear much fruit, because apart from me you can do nothing. (John 15:4–5)

Holiness Is a Process

Jesus' vine-and-branches symbolism reveals holiness as an ongoing organic process. The Holy Spirit takes root in the life of the Christian and begins a growth dynamic. Living out one's baptism is the daily experience of this growth toward Christian maturity. An important insight here is that it is this relationship with Jesus that is the foundation, motivation, and final goal for this journey of faith. *Lumen Gentium* directs the faithful to "use the strength that they have received as a gift from Christ" in order to achieve this Christian maturity. By following Christ's footsteps and seeking God's will in all things, Christians must "devote themselves with all their being to the glory of God and the service of their neighbor" (LG 40).

The journey of holiness is nothing less than moving toward the goal of complete union with God. St. Paul imagines Christian maturity or growing in holiness as a race of faith during which the finish line must always be kept in sight.

> Not that I have already obtained this or have already reached the goal; but I press on to make it my own, because Christ Jesus has made me his own. Beloved, I do not consider that I have made it my own; but this one thing I do: forgetting what lies behind and straining forward to what lies ahead, I press on toward the goal for the prize of the heavenly call of God in Christ Jesus. (Phil 3:12–14)

Christian maturity is best understood as a journey, a process, or, in the case of this passage in Philippians, a marathon race. Holiness does not happen automatically all at once. There are many fits and starts on the journey because of the ongoing human struggle with sin and spiritual weakness. As the relationship with Jesus grows and deepens in intimacy, the fruits of holiness become apparent. And as with any relationship, there are ups and downs, progress and setbacks, successes and failures. This is why an understanding of holiness as a slow maturing in Christ is perhaps the healthiest way to consider it.

In his Letter to the Romans, St. Paul uses an "already–not yet" dynamic to explain progress in the life of grace. Christians are "already saved" because of their baptism and the presence of the Holy Spirit dwelling within. They have already received the free gift of salvation. However, there is still more to come. Christians growing in holiness are "not yet" completely in union with Christ. The grace of God has already been given, but in the organic growth of holiness, new opportunities to allow this grace to permeate every aspect of life are constantly presenting themselves. Already saved and still being saved—in terms of allowing the gift of salvation to be fully realized in one's life—is what the Christian life is all about. St. Paul's dynamic of "already–not yet" is another New Testament teaching that conceives of holiness as a process.

> Therefore, since we are justified by faith, we have peace with God through our Lord Jesus Christ, through whom we have obtained access to this grace in which we stand; and we boast in our hope of sharing the glory of God....Much more surely then, now that we have been justified by his blood, will we be saved through him from the wrath of God. (Rom 5:1–2, 9)

The Second Vatican Council recognized this ongoing progress in holiness as a struggle with sin and imperfection. Every Christian has already been saved, but the struggle with sin and patterns of spiritual weakness are a slow journey to the fullness of salvation. Therefore, the church as a whole is holy but at the same time, since it embraces sinners, is always in need of reform and renewal (LG 8).

The council documents speak eloquently of the "pilgrim Church" on a journey toward full union with God. "Christ summons the Church to continual reformation as she sojourns here on earth. The Church is always in need of this, in so far as she is an institution of men here on earth."[1] This pilgrimage in human history, which reveals the "already–not yet" dynamic of holiness, will come to its fulfillment and completion only in heaven, when all things will be restored (see especially LG 48).

This organic growth in holiness is fueled, in part, by Christian hope. Even when it seems that no spiritual progress is evident, Christian hope provides the patience needed to persevere. The struggle with sin and patterns of bad behavior can be discouraging and draining, but St. Paul says that Christians must rely on hope to sustain them. Endurance in the lifelong journey to Christian maturity is motivated by the Holy Spirit dwelling within.

> I consider that the sufferings of this present time are not
> worth comparing with the glory about to be revealed to
> us...and not only the creation, but we ourselves, who
> have the first fruits of the Spirit, groan inwardly while
> we wait for adoption, the redemption of our bodies. For
> in hope we were saved...if we hope for what we do not
> see, we wait for it with patience. (Rom 8:18, 23–25)

Pope John Paul II, *Christifideles Laici*

The 1988 document on the laity by Pope John Paul II also
takes up this renewed understanding of holiness from the New
Testament. As mentioned in chapter two, the pope explains the
vocation of the laity as flowing from their sacramental identity in
baptism. He also discusses the laity's call to holiness in the light
of the mystery of baptism. "The vocation to holiness must be recognized and lived by the lay faithful....[It] ought to be called an
essential and inseparable element of the new life of Baptism..."
(CFL 17). The pope defines holiness as "the perfection of charity"
(CFL 16), and laypeople are not to be left out of this call since they
are "on equal par with all other members of the Church" and "are
called to holiness" (CFL 16).

Commenting on the council's universal call to holiness, the
pope says that the intention of Vatican II was to bring about a
spiritual renewal of the whole church based on the Gospel. He
goes on to state that this need for spiritual transformation is still
urgent; all Christians must accept St. Peter's invitation to "be holy
in all conduct" (1 Pet 1:15; see CFL 16).

An interesting element of the pope's explanation of holiness is
that it is not simply a moral exhortation directed to Christians.
Instead, he places it in the context of the very nature of the church
itself. That is, as the vine of God, the very nature of the church is to
bear fruit. Bearing the fruit of holiness is not something above and
beyond the duty of ordinary Christians but is an absolute require-
ment of all who are branches on the vine of God (CFL 16).

The reason why holiness is not optional or not an "extra" in
the life of the church is that the success of the church's mission

depends on it. The church carries on the mission of Jesus to spread the kingdom of God and thereby transform the world. This mission is fueled by the Holy Spirit and energized by the fruits of holiness in the lives of all the members of the church. Pope John Paul II states that holiness is actually "a fundamental presupposition and an irreplaceable condition" for mission since it is "the hidden source and the infallible measure of the works of the apostolate" (CFL 17). He grounds his teaching in the Second Vatican Council, which affirmed that the personal holiness of believers contributes to the church's mission to transform the world (LG 40).

In considering their own call to holiness, the lay faithful are continually challenged to avoid the false dichotomy between daily activities and the life of faith. Both the council fathers and Pope John Paul II insist on understanding the laity's call to holiness as being issued in and through the very stuff of daily life. The messiness of life in the world is actually itself an invitation to grow closer to Christ. Christian maturity does not take the laity out of "the world." Rather, laypersons' ordinary lives are the God-given opportunities to produce the fruits of Christian holiness, and neither family concerns nor any other secular matters are to be excluded from responses to the invitation to holiness (CFL 17).

Conclusion

The New Testament teaching on holiness begins with Jesus, the holy one of God. His exhortation to holiness flows from his divine identity and is itself an invitation to relationship. Through baptism, believers enter into a covenantal relationship with God in the power of the Holy Spirit. This new identity as God's holy people is to be lived out in daily life. The principle here is that "being comes before doing." The gift of the Holy Spirit in baptism comes before the challenge of living it out in concrete ways; that is, being holy because of God's free gift of salvation and the indwelling of the Holy Spirit "comes before" the "doing" or living out of the Christian call: "For this is the will of God, your sanctification" (1 Thess 4:3).

In summary, the biblical theology of holiness from the Old and New Testaments is the foundation of the Second Vatican

Council's teaching on the universal vocation of all the Christian faithful to holiness. No one is left out of the dignity of the call to spiritual maturity. All the Christian faithful are not only invited but also are obliged to strive for the holiness and perfection proper to their own state in life (LG 42).

Reflection Questions

1. What immediately strikes you about the "universal call to holiness"?

2. Explain both the gift and challenge of holiness.

3. How is the person of the Holy Spirit the source and power of the holiness of all believers?

4. Name a few personal examples of the process of holiness and Christian maturity in your own faith journey.

5. According to Pope John Paul II, why must holiness be the energy for mission?

CHAPTER FOUR

The Mission of the Laity

Mission—Not for the Clergy Only

The Second Vatican Council's teaching on the role of the laity in the mission of the church was yet another dimension of the "New Pentecost" envisioned by Pope John XXIII. A rediscovery of the sacraments of baptism and confirmation as "mission sacraments" led to a renewed understanding of the role of the laity in spreading the kingdom of God through word and deed. The old vision of a passive laity, mere recipients of the ministry of the clergy, gave way to a fresh appreciation of the responsibility of the lay faithful in the mission of the church. Vatican II replaced the old "pay, pray, and obey" model with a biblically-based mandate to the laity to renew the world for the sake of Christ.

Once again the Holy Spirit seemed to be prompting the church to rediscover the reality of its own inner life and mission as found in the New Testament. By offering a revitalizing appreciation for Christ's call to mission, the council challenged the laity to become more aware of their shared responsibility in the overall activity of the church. The Body of Christ has many parts, none of which is purely passive! Baptism and confirmation empower for mission both within the church and in the world. Ordained persons are not expected to assume the entire responsibility for the church's salvific mission but must also rely on the unique contributions to be made by the lay faithful (LG 30).

Traditionally, the average layperson considered the mission of the church to be entrusted to the hierarchy alone. This view was actually grounded in a popular misperception even shared by the hierarchy themselves and was based on a deficient understanding of mission that, once again, had the sacrament of holy orders as the center of its vision. Holy orders was perceived to be the sacrament that empowered one for mission. This view gave the apostolate of the church to the hierarchy alone and laypersons could, at best, simply cooperate in this apostolate. The lay faithful could only have a derivative role dependent upon the mission of the hierarchy—and this cooperation had to be organized, mandated, and controlled by the clergy.

This traditional understanding was based on the assumption that Jesus entrusted his mission to the apostles and therefore only the successors of the apostles were responsible for it. In the commissioning scenes of the four Gospels (Matthew 28, Mark 16, Luke 24, John 20) and Acts 1, it is indeed the apostles who are charged with continuing the work of the risen Lord. Therefore, it seemed from these passages that only the hierarchy of the church, the successors of the apostles, was mandated to fulfill this mission. So, it must be admitted that there is a certain logic to this position.

This older theology of mission, however, was limited by its exclusive focus on these few commissioning scenes in the Gospels and in Acts. The fathers of the Second Vatican Council revisited the teaching of St. Paul on the theology of baptism and the gifts of the Holy Spirit given to every believer and in so doing corrected this old view. Every member of the church receives the Holy Spirit and is therefore in some way responsible for fulfilling the mission of Jesus. The mandate for mission is not only given to the hierarchy; the laity also share in the responsibility and are sent on this mission by the Lord himself. The church is characterized by "a diversity of ministry but a oneness of mission" in which the laity "share in the priestly, prophetic, and royal office of Christ" by fulfilling, in their own proper way, the church's purpose of spreading the kingdom and announcing Christ's saving redemption to all (AA 2).

As seen in chapter one, the council corrected this traditional view of mission by putting baptism back in the center of the church's life. By appropriating St. Paul's teaching concerning mission, Vatican II breathed new life into the theological understanding of the role and function of the lay faithful.

> Now there are varieties of gifts, but the same Spirit;
> and there are varieties of services, but the same Lord;
> and there are varieties of activities, but it is the same
> God who activates all of them in everyone. To each is
> given the manifestation of the Spirit for the common
> good....For in the one Spirit we were all baptized into
> one body...and we were all made to drink of one Spirit.
> (1 Cor 12:4–7, 13)

St. Paul's image of the church as the body of Christ high-lights the fact that each of the members of the church has different but complementary roles to play in the one overall mission. This reality rests on the theological notion of the communion of the church discussed in chapter two. The church is a communion of the baptized who share a baptismal dignity and complementary roles in the mission of the risen Lord. The lay faithful do not receive this mission, therefore, by delegation from the hierarchy but by their sacramental identity of baptism and confirmation.

Confirmation and Mission

One interesting feature of the teaching of Vatican II concerning the mission of the laity is the theology of the sacrament of confirmation. The council texts that speak of the mission of the lay faithful link confirmation with baptism. The characters of these two sacraments equip and empower the laity for mission in the church and in the world. Here the teaching of the council uses the principle that being comes before doing or that identity in the church comes before role or function. That is, who the laity *are* in the church determines their role or mission. The lay faithful are fully members of the Body of Christ, the communion of the church, through their baptism and confirmation. Their role flows from this sacramental identity. The marks or characters of baptism and confirmation, then, give the lay faithful their active role in the life and mission of the church.

Traditional theology understands confirmation as a fuller, deeper outpouring of the Holy Spirit in power. Of course, as we saw in chapter two, the Holy Spirit is received first of all in baptism. The baptized are temples of the Holy Spirit, who dwells within them. As Jesus promised, the believer will have rivers of living water flowing within to quench the thirst for salvation.

> Let anyone who is thirsty come to me, and let the one who believes in me drink. As the scripture has said, "Out of the believer's heart shall flow rivers of living water." Now he said this about the Spirit, which believers in him were to receive. (John 7:37–39)

Confirmation releases this Spirit in power in an even more profound way. This sacrament is usually associated with the event of Pentecost, when the apostles, the Virgin Mary, and the early followers of Jesus, who were gathered in prayer, experienced the Spirit's presence in a new way (Acts 2:1–41). Pentecost is the birthday of the Church, the founding event of the people of God, just as the Mount Sinai experience was the foundation of the people of Yahweh in Exodus 19. At Mount Sinai the sacred assembly of the twelve Hebrew tribes experienced wind, fire, and the trembling of the earth as God came to his people in an intimate way. The Hebrews sealed a covenant with the God who had saved them from the bondage of slavery in Egypt. This covenant gave them both an identity and a mission. They were to be God's special possession, a kingdom of priests, and a holy nation. Their mission was to listen to God's voice and follow his covenant and commandments. This would set them apart from other nations and peoples.

Pentecost is the new Mount Sinai event, since the early Christians were gathered in prayer and experienced a loud noise, a strong wind, and fire, as God the Holy Spirit came to them in an intimate way. The new covenant sealed through the blood of Jesus himself formed a new community of those saved from the powers of sin and death. Pentecost is a foundational event that empowers a new people of God, and this spirit-filled community is sent on mission, equipped with spiritual gifts.

> ...[T]hey were all together in one place. And suddenly from heaven there came a sound like the rush of a violent

wind, and it filled the entire house where they were sitting. Divided tongues, as of fire, appeared among them, and a tongue rested on each of them. All of them were filled with the Holy Spirit and began to speak in other languages, as the Spirit gave them ability. (Acts 2:1–4)

The Pentecost sacrament, then, is confirmation. The gifts of the Holy Spirit are released in a profound way and these gifts are always directed toward mission in some manner. The sacramental character of confirmation deputes the believer for public service, public witness, and public mission. In the past, it was even taught that confirmation provided the grace for martyrdom, if need be. The Second Vatican Council teaches that confirmation binds the faithful more perfectly to the church and endows them with the special strength of the Holy Spirit in order to fulfill their obligation of witnessing to Christ and spreading the faith (LG 11).

The New Testament gives evidence of this experience of a deeper outpouring of the Spirit in power in a few stories from Acts. The apostles pray over individuals who were already baptized to receive the Holy Spirit in a profound way. This experience, subsequent to baptism, later developed into the sacrament of confirmation. The Acts of the Apostles describes it thus:

Now when the apostles at Jerusalem heard that Samaria had accepted the word of God, they sent Peter and John to them. The two went down and prayed for them that they might receive the Holy Spirit (for as yet the Spirit had not come upon any of them; they had only been baptized in the name of the Lord Jesus). Then Peter and John laid their hands on them, and they received the Holy Spirit. (Acts 8:14–17)

Baptized Christians, like these new believers mentioned in Acts, experience a deeper release of the Holy Spirit for the sake of the church's mission. The Holy Spirit's presence not only gives the members of the church their identity, but it also equips them to act on Christ's behalf. Confirmation allows believers to be "qualified" and empowered to act in the name of Jesus for the glory of God the Father. Usually, the effect of confirmation is described as making one a mature and responsible Christian. This flows from the graces of the sacrament and the individual's cooperation with these graces. This adult moral strength is evidenced by actions, attitudes, priorities, words, and lifestyle. The graces of confirmation are made clear when the Holy Spirit energizes laypersons' inner convictions and everyday activities.

Vatican II appealed to this understanding of confirmation in its teaching on the mission of the laity. Baptized and confirmed, the lay faithful are full sharers in the one mission of the church. The graces of the Holy Spirit mark, equip, and energize laypeople to live and profess their Christian faith in a public way. The power of Pentecost motivates the whole church to spread the kingdom of God through word and deed. The anointing of the Spirit through confirmation is "to equip the saints for the work of ministry, for building up the body of Christ" (Eph 4:12).

Charisms and the Mission of the Laity

The discussions of the council fathers about the mission of the laity also raised the issue of the availability of charisms or gifts of the Holy Spirit. Were the gifts of the Holy Spirit only for the first-century church? Or did every age of church history see the flourishing of charisms or gifts in the lives of Christians? Was the availability of these charisms restricted to the establishment and beginnings of the church or were they necessary to animate the mission of the church in every age? Moreover, if these gifts of the Spirit were a necessary part of the life of the church, who was eligible to receive them?

The question of charisms became an important topic at Vatican II because it was linked to other basic questions about the identity and function of the laity. These include the theology of baptism, the call to holiness, and the reality of the church as a communion of believers who share a common dignity and equality in the church. As we have already seen, the shift in thinking about the church caused by putting baptism back at the center had important repercussions in the theology of the laity, so that it was no longer the sacrament of holy orders communicating gifts of the Holy Spirit to ordained persons who had an exclusive responsibility for the mission of the church.

On the floor of the council, Cardinal Suenens of Belgium gave a now-famous speech that called for the consideration of a theology of charisms in light of the teaching of St. Paul in the New Testament. He stressed that the gifts of the Holy Spirit were valid for every age of the church and were given to build up the Body of Christ. Rather than being peripheral or unessential, these charisms are absolutely vital for the church's inner life and mission. St. Paul did not present the church as a mere administrative structure; instead, the New Testament presents the Christian community as a web of gifts, charisms, and ministries. The Holy Spirit is given to every believer, according to St. Paul. Therefore, maintained Cardinal Suenens, the presence of charisms in the lives of the laity needed to be explored. As a result of his intervention, the council did indeed undertake a more extended and concrete treatment of this topic.

The presence of charisms in the lives of the saints down through the centuries has always been recognized. Canonized saints are honored because of their lives of outstanding holiness and their extraordinary exercise of spiritual gifts in their vocation and mission. While these examples of Christian heroic virtue are certainly inspiring, at times a false impression can be given that this type of intense Christian existence is beyond the reach of the ordinary layperson. Those formally recognized as saints seem to be far removed from the ordinary lives of lay men and women living in the world. Often celibate, ascetic miracle workers, the saints and martyrs of the church's liturgical calendar, especially those who lived in the first millennium, "leave the world" to follow Christ. Not only does this type of approach make holiness seem like it is only for a select few; it also gives the false impression that charisms are only for the elite in the church.

Once again Vatican II reclaimed the teaching of the New Testament in order to rebalance this misperception concerning the presence of charisms in the lives of laypersons. By a fresh reading of St. Paul, the council fathers were able to assert that the sacraments of baptism and especially confirmation bestow gifts of the Holy Spirit on everyone. The recentering of the teaching on charisms in the theology of baptism and confirmation had a profound impact on the reality of the mission of the laity in the church and in the world. As *Lumen Gentium* declared, the Spirit distributes his gifts and graces as he wills so that all Christians in their own unique way may be thus prepared to contribute to the renewal and building up of the church (LG 12).

The People of God Have a Mission

The discussions and debates over the mission of the laity mentioned above resulted in the official teaching found in *Lumen Gentium* and *Apostolicam Actuositatem*. By reclaiming the biblical foundations for a theology of mission, the council was able to move beyond the old view of mission that only included the clergy. Far from being the responsibility of only those in holy orders, the mission of the church was explained as being the task of every member of the people of God. No one is left out of this call to build up the Body of Christ. The lay faithful, too, are called upon "to expend all their energy for the growth of the Church and its continuous sanctification, since this very energy is a gift of the Creator and a blessing of the Redeemer" (LG 33).

The nature and sources for the mission of the laity are outlined in a fundamental way in *Lumen Gentium* 33 and *Apostolicam Actuositatem* 2 and 3. These passages begin by explaining the renewed understanding of the mission of the laity in terms of "where it fits" in the life of the church. A real theological breakthrough is the description of the lay apostolate as "a participation in the salvific mission of the Church itself" (LG 33)—that is, it is not simply a sharing or cooperation in the apostolate of the hierarchy. The church is a living body, and as such has no passive parts: as with all living bodies, so, too, in the body of Christ, each member is called to make his or her proper contribution to its development (AA 2).

Thus the lay faithful enjoy a greater responsibility than they did in the old model. Instead, they now have an essential role to play in the mission of the church and must apply all the powers they have received for the growth of the church and its continual sancti-fication, or maturing in holiness. Laypersons have both the right and the duty to participate in the church's mission in the world and to contribute to its inner life and organization.

BAPTISM AND CONFIRMATION

The description of the theological basis or justification for the mission of the laity from Vatican II is rooted in sacramental identity. The sacraments of baptism and confirmation empower the lay faithful for their mission in the church and in the world. As seen above, through this appeal to these two sacraments the coun-cil moved away from the old view that mission was only connected to the sacrament of holy orders. *Apostolicam Actuositatem* adds that the sacraments, especially holy Eucharist, communicate and nourish the charity toward God and humanity that is the soul of mission (AA 3).

SECULAR CHARACTER

The council fathers maintained that the laity's role is unique within the overall mission of the church (see especially LG 33 and AA 2). The laity's relationship to the world, their living in the midst of the world and its concerns, gives their mission a special character; God calls them to "exercise their apostolate in the world like leaven, with the ardor of the spirit of Christ" (AA 2).

The council highlights the secular quality of the activity of the laity in the church and in the world. That does not make the laity less holy, or "worldly" in the negative biblical meaning of the term. On the contrary, the council affirms that there are certain circum-stances and places where the church can only be the salt of the earth and the light of the world through the laity. The lay faithful, because of their secular character, make the church present "and operative in those places and circumstances where only through them can it become the salt of the earth" (LG 33).

This stress on the secular character of the laity serves to affirm the tremendous value of their ordinary lives. As mentioned in chapter two, the council fathers took seriously the everyday activities of laypeople and, in so doing, gave dignity and meaning to every aspect of their daily existence. By connecting the call to holiness and the call to mission with the secular character of the lay faithful, Vatican II gave spiritual significance to their normal lives in the family, workplace, school, and society. The regular activities of the laity are the means by which they can fulfill the mission of the church.

This is what the council means when it uses the phrase *living instruments* in reference to the secular character. The laity live out the mission of the church in the very web of their existence. There is to be no division between the private lives of the lay faithful and the public witness of their faith. Each layperson has specific gifts bestowed by Christ by which to be "a witness and a living instrument of the mission of the Church itself" (LG 33).

COLLABORATION WITH THE HIERARCHY

Another aspect of Vatican II's teaching on the mission of the laity has to do with their role in the inner life of the church. What sorts of roles can lay men and women take on within the internal workings of the church? The council uses the phrase *direct cooperation* in explaining the collaboration between laity and the hierarchy within the inner life of the people of God. This goes beyond the basic form of apostolate or mission to which all laypeople are called; instead, it is a form of participation in the church's mission to which only some laypersons, according to their circumstances, would be called. Specifically, it is some sort of organized apostolic activity that is carried out under the direction of the hierarchy.

In making this point, *Lumen Gentium* does not list specific forms that this cooperation with the hierarchy might take; but it is interesting that once again the council is reclaiming the teaching and example of St. Paul (see LG 33). Men and women who worked with St. Paul in the promotion of the Gospel are cited as the precedent for laypersons' roles and responsibilities within the inner workings of the church today. Apparently there are numerous forms of this direct cooperation, since the council says that the laity can be called in "different ways." Indeed, in the forty-plus years since Vatican II, there has been a marked increase in lay roles within the worship life, administration, charitable out-reach, and educational activities of the church.

In acknowledging a diversity of ministry within a oneness of mission (AA 2), the council goes on to affirm an even more inti-mate service that the laity can fulfill in the church. Laypersons have the capacity to exercise certain functions if they are deputed by the hierarchy. This is a much more formal reference to what today is the reality of lay ecclesial ministry in the church. The council then speaks of "offices" that can be fulfilled by the lay faithful. This is a technical term that refers to duties or functions that belong properly to the hierarchy but that can be entrusted to laypersons, if necessary, for a spiritual purpose.

The council affirms that the laity have a capacity to fulfill these ecclesiastical functions for a spiritual purpose because of their membership in the people of God (LG 33). In other words, laypersons who are engaged in these roles are not doing something for which they have no competence or mission, but are carrying out these duties on the basis of their sacramental identity through baptism and confirmation. Because they have been baptized and confirmed and share in the mission of the church itself, they can cooperate with the hierarchy in exercising certain ministries.

By stressing the diversity of ministries within a unity of mis-sion, the council underlines the basic equality, yet functional diver-sity of all the members of the church. This unity is not meant to be uniformity; rather, the church exercises a diversity of ministries within the one purpose of spreading the kingdom of God. In fact, the diversity of ministries within the church is itself a unifying force, since the diversity of functions aims at building up the church as a whole. The richness of the church lies not only in the difference between the roles, but also in the convergence of these roles at the service of one and the same mission.

CHARISMS AND VIRTUES

Besides the sacraments of baptism and confirmation, the Second Vatican Council also highlighted the gifts of the Holy Spirit and the theological virtues as the motivation for the mission of the laity. By stressing this spiritual foundation for the mission of the lay faithful, the council is teaching that mission is not to be understood as simply a job or task. Instead, the mission of the church is a supernatural enterprise that is fueled, guided, and preserved by the Holy Spirit itself. The gifts or charisms of the Spirit, along with the supernatural virtues, are, therefore, indispensable in any understanding of the role of the laity in the church and in the world. Even the most elementary charisms carry with them the right and the duty to use them in the church and the world for the good of others and for building up the church, "in the freedom of the Holy Spirit who 'breathes where He wills' (John 3:8). This should be done by the laity in communion with their brothers in Christ, especially with their pastors" (AA 3).

This section of *Apostolicam Actuositatem* is based upon the New Testament teaching concerning charisms from 1 Peter 4, 1 Corinthians 12, and Ephesians 4. Basically, these passages affirm that every member of the church receives gifts of the Holy Spirit for the building up of the Body of Christ. The council maintains that the reception of these charisms brings with it rights and duties to exercise them. The duty or responsibility to use these gifts is that of being open and responding to the graces bestowed by the Holy Spirit. It is expected that the laity will yield to the power of the Holy Spirit in their lives of service to the mission of the church. And the right that flows from these spiritual gifts is to have them recognized and discerned by the pastors of the church, "not to extinguish the Spirit but to test all things and hold for what is good (cf. 1 Thess 5:12, 19, 21)" (AA 3).

The supernatural virtues of faith, hope, and charity are also part of the spiritual foundation of the mission of the laity. These virtues, which are poured into the hearts of believers by the Holy Spirit, are a motivating force for their role in the spread of the kingdom through word and deed. At a very basic level, it is the living out of these virtues that characterizes the Christian life. The embodiment of faith, hope, and love in ordinary events and experiences is itself a way of participating in the mission of the church. These three virtues are supernatural empowerments for mission, and charity, "the Lord's greatest commandment," impels all the faithful "to promote the glory of God through the coming of His kingdom" (AA 3).

This obligation to work for the glory of God through the coming of his kingdom is given to every Christian believer. It is not an additional responsibility for only certain members of the church, for example, the hierarchy. The laity are given charisms and theological virtues that are the inner driving force of their mission. They have at their disposal the power of Pentecost to permeate their daily lives and make them living instruments of the church's mission in the world.

Lumen Gentium and *Apostolicam Actuositatem* both issue a challenge to the laity to channel their apostolic energy received in baptism and confirmation into the spread of the kingdom of God through evangelization and transformation of the world. In the church there is a diversity of ministry, but a unity of mission. The infusion and distribution of the theological virtues and gifts of the Holy Spirit to the laity equip and empower them for this saving activity, to which they are invited by the Lord himself.

Pope John Paul II, *Christifideles Laici*

Christifideles Laici also takes up this renewed, New Testament-based understanding of mission from Vatican II. The pope begins with a reminder that the lay faithful have been summoned by Christ himself to labor in the vineyard. This invitation is renewed each day as they grow closer to Christ so that as they recognize that what is Christ's is also theirs (Phil 2:5), they might associate themselves with Christ in his saving mission (CFL 2).

The Lord's invitation to mission comes in the sacrament of baptism and is then deepened in the empowerment of confirmation. The mission of the church, says the pope, is a continuation of the threefold mission of Jesus as priest, prophet, and king. These three aspects of the mission of Jesus and the participation of the laity in them are outlined in section 14 of the document.

PRIEST, PROPHET, AND KING

Relying on the teaching of Vatican II, Pope John Paul summarizes some of the essential points of the laity's participation in all three aspects. First, the priestly aspect of Jesus' own mission is highlighted in light of his self-offering sacrifice on the cross. Jesus' death is the once-and-for-all sacrifice offered for the sins of all. His cross becomes the altar of sacrifice and his shed blood seals the new covenant with God. The baptized are incorporated into Christ and therefore share this priestly aspect of his mission. By offering up their own daily lives as a sacrifice of praise and service, the lay faithful participate in this priestly aspect of Jesus' mission. In doing so, they consecrate the world itself to God: "Incorporated in Jesus Christ, the baptized are united to him and to his sacrifice in the offering they make of themselves and their daily activities (Romans 12:1–2)" (CFL 14).

The second aspect of Jesus' mission is the prophetic call he lived. Jesus proclaimed the kingdom of God in word and deed. Jesus broke the power of evil by his authoritative teaching, his healing of sickness, and his exorcizing of demons. He was a prophet mighty in speech and action. The baptized share in the grace of his word and the new life that comes from the power of his Gospel. The laity share in the prophetic mission of Jesus by witnessing to the word in big and small ways in their daily lives; this includes expressing "patiently and courageously in the contradictions of the present age their hope of future glory even through the framework of their secular life" (CFL 14).

The kingly aspect of the mission of Jesus is the third dimension that the pope highlights in his understanding of the laity's share in these three offices. The royal mission of Jesus as Messiah aims at making the kingdom of God a reality in all of creation. This kingdom, not a political reality but a spiritual reign of grace and the triumph of God's love over every kind of evil and alienation, has the hallmarks of truth, justice, love, and eternal peace. It is God's reign over his creation and is therefore a cosmic reality. The resurrection of Jesus begins this cosmic reconciliation of all things into the fullness of God's reign. The baptized participate in this ongoing reconciliation as they spread the kingdom of God in history. The pope exhorts the laity to take up this spiritual combat in their personal lives and to order creation to God's reign. In taking up this challenge, he points out, the lay faithful "share in the exercise of the power with which the Risen Christ draws all things to himself..." (CFL 14).

BAPTISM AND CONFIRMATION

Sacramental identity, which is so important in the council's theology of the mission of the laity, figures prominently in *Christifideles Laici*. The spiritual energy or power that enables the laity to participate actively in the threefold mission of Jesus as priest, prophet, and king comes from the sacramental life and communion of the church. The source of this participation is found in baptism, "its further development in Confirmation and its realization and dynamic sustenance in the Holy Eucharist" (CFL 14.) The pope encourages clergy to recognize and promote these ministries, offices, and roles of the lay faithful which are founded in the sacraments of baptism and confirmation as well as, for many of them, in the sacrament of matrimony (CFL 23).

SECULAR CHARACTER

The communion of the church is the source and empowerment for this consecrating, proclaiming, and ordering mission. "Precisely because it derives *from* Church *communion*, the sharing of the lay faithful in the threefold mission of Christ requires that it be lived and realized *in communion* and *for the increase of communion itself*" (CFL 14). The particular challenge for the laity, of course, is to allow this communion-driven mission to unfold in the very ordinary events of daily life. This threefold mission gives a new perspective on the seemingly mundane activities of laypeople. The temporal activities of the laity can become the very means for the priestly, prophet, and royal mission of Jesus to be fulfilled.

The unique contribution that the lay faithful make to the mission of the church is the living out of their secular character in an intentional way so that ordinary events become the means for the mission of Jesus to be realized. Politics, society, economics, culture, human love, family life, their professions, and even suffering—all these are among the arenas in which the laity exercise their mission to evangelize (CFL 23). The mission of Jesus permeates every aspect of the lives of laypeople so that the human relationships and the events of everyday become the very instruments and opportunities for the spread of the kingdom.

COLLABORATION WITH THE HIERARCHY

Christifideles Laici stresses the complementarity of the ministries, offices, and roles of the laity and those of the clergy, and points to the role of the pastors of the church in recognizing and promoting these ecclesial activities of the laity, which are grounded in their baptismal identity. As Vatican II taught, laypeople can be called into a closer collaboration with the pastoral ministry of the clergy to fulfill the mission of the church. When pastoral necessities require, the clergy can entrust to laypersons certain offices and functions that are connected to their pastoral ministry but do not require the sacrament of orders, and are rooted in the baptismal identity of the laity (CFL 23).

This collaboration between the laity and the clergy in ministry is to be experienced first of all in the liturgy. The liturgical life of the church is where the renewed theology of the mission of the laity can be seen perhaps most clearly. No longer considered as simply the work of the priest, the liturgy is now understood as the work of the whole assembly, who all celebrate together through a diversity of roles and functions. The conscious and active participation of the lay faithful in the liturgy forms the basis of their collaboration with the clergy in the wider pastoral ministry of the church insofar as "there is a natural transition from an effective involvement of the lay faithful in the liturgical action to that of announcing the word of God and pastoral care" (CFL 23).

CHARISMS

The papal exhortation devotes an entire section (24) to the topic of gifts of the Holy Spirit, or charisms. Affirming the teaching of Vatican II, the pope states that within the communion of the church, the Holy Spirit bestows diverse charisms and ministries. These gifts of the Spirit are for every believer, as the New Testament makes clear. The richness in the diversity of these charisms within the unity of the communion of the church demonstrates both the freedom of the Holy Spirit and the response of the Spirit to the various needs of the church in every age (CFL 24).

The usefulness for these charisms of the Holy Spirit for the church is threefold, according to the pope. He states that the charisms are given by the Spirit to edify the church, to insure the well-being of humanity, and to meet the needs of the world. These promptings of grace, which can be given to an individual believer or shared by others, are also the source of ministries and services in the church. "They are in fact a singularly rich source of grace for the vitality of the apostolate and for the holiness of the whole Body of Christ..." (CFL 24).

In order for these charisms to be fully realized and effective, the discernment of the Spirit is always necessary. The pope calls for the careful discernment of the gifts of the Holy Spirit, which will ensure that they will work together in their diversity and complementarity for the common good. This discernment is carried out by the pastors of the church, who are charged not to extinguish the Spirit, but to test all things and to hold fast to that which is good (1 Thess 5:12, 19–21).

Pope John Paul II presents the church as an organic communion, characterized by the presence of both diversity and complementarity of vocations, ministries, charisms, and responsibilities. Within this communion, the laity are characterized by their sacramental identity and secular character. Through baptism and confirmation, laypeople participate with all of the faithful in the threefold offices of Jesus and therefore share in his priestly, prophetic, and kingly mission. The lay faithful, consequently, have a right and duty to participate in the mission of the church and their roles will be determined by their specific vocations and the charisms they have received from the Holy Spirit.

Conclusion

This brief analysis of *Lumen Gentium* and *Apostolicam Actuositatem* from Vatican II, as well as Pope John Paul II's exhortation *Christifideles Laici*, demonstrates the breakthrough that happened regarding the theology of the mission of the laity. This changed understanding of the basis, nature, and scope of the mission of the lay faithful is evidence of a true renewal in the church's teaching. Indeed, these documents form part of the impetus and inspiration for a new age of the laity in terms of their active involvement in the saving mission of the church.

Jesus calls all believers—not only a select few—to join him in his mission. This summons is a call to a relationship that bears fruit in daily life. From the communion of believers with Jesus and with one another, this mission is generated and sustained. As John's gospel teaches, "You did not choose me but I chose you. And I appointed you to go and bear fruit, fruit that will last" (John 15:16). The vocation of all the baptized is to be a "branch on the vine," who is Jesus himself. Bearing fruit is the mission of every branch. But the mission cannot be achieved unless the relationship of remaining in Jesus is lived out. Apart from a living, dynamic relationship with him, a communion of love, bearing fruit is impossible.

> Abide in me as I abide in you. Just as the branch cannot bear fruit by itself unless it abides in the vine, neither can you unless you abide in me. I am the vine, you are the branches. Those who abide in me and I in them bear much fruit, because apart from me you can do nothing. (John 15:4–5)

Reflection Questions

1. Jesus was sent on mission by the Father in the power of the Holy Spirit. How is this original sending still present in the church today?

2. What would be some effective ways of preparing young people for confirmation in light of the theology of mission from Vatican II?

3. How did the Second Vatican Council reclaim a spirituality of charisms or gifts, and how does that affect the laity?

4. What does true collaboration in mission look like in the church?

CHAPTER FIVE

The Ministry of the Laity in the Church

An Unforeseen Grace

The Second Vatican Council's renewed theology of the vocation and mission of the laity had an almost immediate impact on the life of the church. The age of the laity had dawned. The fresh appreciation for the sacrament of baptism and the call to mission flowing from the sacrament of confirmation became the occasion for laypersons to realize their roles and responsibilities in the life of the church. But one grace of the new Pentecost that was certainly unexpected by the council fathers was the phenomenon of lay ministry in the church.

While it is true that a few passages from the council documents mentioned the possibility of inviting laypeople to certain forms of ministry within the church, the main focus of the role of the laity was in the everyday world. Most of the exhortations of the council to the lay faithful concerned their responsibility to transform the temporal order for the sake of Christ. Secular affairs rather than internal church ministries were the focal point of the apostolate of the laity. Therefore, the rise in lay ministry almost immediately after Vatican II was unforeseen even by the council fathers themselves.

But rather than consider lay ministry in the church as a new development of the twentieth century, it is more helpful to reflect on the teaching of the New Testament for a proper understanding of this phenomenon. This unforeseen grace was actually a revival of the notion of shared ministry in the New Testament. In the earliest days of the church, service to the Body of Christ was a collaborative endeavor. Once again, the experience and teaching of St. Paul is instructive. The council affirms that there is historical precedence for lay involvement in ministry coming from the activities of St. Paul himself (cf. Acts 18:18, 26; Rom 16:3). Like the women and men who helped St. Paul, so today "the laity with the right apostolic attitude supply what is lacking to their brethren and refresh the spirit of pastors and of the rest of the faithful (cf. 1 Cor 16:17–18)" (AA 10).

In his letters in the New Testament, St. Paul mentions the names of men and women who are his coworkers in the Gospel (Romans 16, Philippians 4). Important figures such as Aquila, Prisca, Junia, Phoebe, Clement, and Timothy are just a sampling of the people who shared in St. Paul's ministry as coworkers in the Lord. The council looked to this ministerial practice of St. Paul to shape its own teaching on the collaboration of the laity in ministry when it affirmed that the laity can be called in various ways to a more direct form of cooperation in the mission of the hierarchy (LG 33).

St. Paul's theology of the church as the Body of Christ and his robust theology of charisms are the basis for his conviction that the ministry of the Gospel is a shared, collaborative endeavor. The Holy Spirit's power is at work in the expansion of the church. The gifts of the Holy Spirit flow into and sustain any ministry in the life of the church. The community, although one Body in Christ, has gifts that differ according to the graces given to each member. "For as in one body we have many members, and not all the members have the same function, so we, who are many, are one body in Christ, and individually we are members one of another" (Rom 12:4–6).

This New Testament teaching helps in any consideration of the explosion of lay ministries after the council. Indeed, St. Paul seems to presume that the Spirit-filled life should flow into activity on behalf of the Gospel. "We have gifts that differ according to the grace given to us: prophecy, in proportion to faith; ministry, in ministering; the teacher, in teaching; the exhorter, in exhortation; the giver, in generosity; the leader, in diligence; the compassionate, in cheerfulness" (Rom 12:6–8). God's grace in the Holy Spirit leads to charisms and charisms lead to ministry and these ministries build up the life of the church from within. Once again the Holy Spirit seemed to be prompting the church to rediscover the reality of its own inner life and mission as found in the New Testament.

Lay Ministry in Conciliar Teaching

While it is true that the Second Vatican Council most often speaks of the mission or apostolate of the laity, there are several passages that use the term *ministry* in relation to the lay faithful. These instances, though relatively few, are significant in view of the developments over the past forty years in the inner life and ministry of the church. These passages do not provide a fully developed theology of lay ministry, but they *can* provide insight into how the council fathers were considering the role of the laity within the internal life of the church. According to the council, there are some instances when members of the lay faithful are called upon to cooperate more closely with the apostolate of the hierarchy and exercise roles that can properly be called ministries. The council even makes provisions for situations of persecution or the shortage of clergy when the laity can be commissioned to supply for certain functions that are ordinarily reserved to the clergy. Of course, the laity cannot celebrate Mass or hear confessions, but they can certainly be deputed to baptize, witness marriages, preach, and distribute the Eucharist. In whatever situations they find themselves, each member of the lay faithful is called "to cooperate in the external spread and the dynamic growth of the Kingdom of Christ in the world" (LG 35).

Sacrosanctum Concilium, the Second Vatican Council's Constitution on the Liturgy, says that servers, lectors, commentators, and choir members are performing a true ministry in the church. According to the council, they "ought, therefore, to discharge their office with the sincere piety and decorum demanded by so exalted a ministry and rightly expected of them by God's people" (SC 29, See also 35, 112, and 122).

Gravissimum Educationis, the Declaration on Christian Education, teaches that lay women and men who are involved in catechesis or formal religious instruction are also exercising a true ministry. Laypeople who teach in Catholic schools or give religious instructions to children who attend public schools are engaged in apostolic action that provides spiritual aid to their students.[1] "The work of these teachers, this sacred synod declares, is in the real sense of the word an apostolate most suited to and necessary for our times and at once a true service offered to society" (GE 8).

Missionary activities are also open to the laity and are considered a church ministry by the council. In its discussion of the proper training of missionaries in *Ad Gentes*, the Decree on the Church's Missionary Activity, the council notes that "...all missionaries— priests, Brothers, Sisters, and lay folk—each according to their own state, should be prepared and trained...their doctrinal training should be so planned that it takes in both the universality of the Church and the diversity of the world's nations. This holds for all of their studies by which they are prepared for the exercise of the ministry."[2] This decree also mentions the ministry of those lay men who are not ordained but who perform works proper to deacons, such as teaching catechism, practicing charity in social or relief work, or even presiding over communities in the name of the pastor (AG 26).

Finally, the council uses the word *ministry* in a rather fluid way in *Gaudium et Spes*, the Pastoral Constitution on the Church in the Modern World. Almost any kind of services, including activities promoting peace, justice, or the defense of human life, are considered ministries and are normally considered the tasks of the laity (GS 38, 51).

While these passages from documents of the Second Vatican Council are significant because they use the term *ministry* in relation to the laity, it must be admitted that it is impossible to derive a full-blown theology of lay ministry from the teachings of the council. There is no systematic treatment of the theology of ministry as applied to the laity in the conciliar documents. The council fathers could not fully anticipate the movements of the Holy Spirit in the new age of the laity, nor should they have been expected to. Instead, what should be appreciated is the breakthrough in the renewed theology of mission and charisms as applied to the lay faithful. This rediscovery of the teachings of St. Paul and his experiences of ministry was enough to orient the church in a new direction in its teaching on its own inner life and mission.

The Care of Souls and the Laity

The closer involvement of the laity in the mission of the church resulted in a flowering of new projects and activities. These efforts were the result of the lay faithful living out their vocations empowered by the dynamism of the Holy Spirit after Vatican II. The new age of the laity prompted many to channel their energies into the building up of the life of the church from within. Volunteerism and activism flourished as many lay women and men began to take up their rightful role in the church. No longer treated as children, the laity began to enjoy a maturity and autonomy within the mission of the church.

Referring to the diversity of ministry but oneness of mission in the church, the council fathers stated that the lay faithful share in their own way in the mission of the people of God in the church and in the world (AA 2). The areas of lay involvement in the mission of the church soon after the council included the liturgy, catechesis, evangelization, administration, and charitable endeavors. Traditionally these activities had been restricted to the clergy and religious. But now the lay faithful were being invited into the care of souls, a phrase that was virtually never used in relation to the laity before Vatican II.

The traditional understanding of pastoral ministry was that the care of souls was the responsibility of the clergy, and laypeople were simply its passive recipients. But the council moved away from this approach and instead invited the laity to a fuller participation in the care of souls themselves in such areas as the teaching of Christian doctrine and certain liturgical functions (AA 24).

The laity, indeed, share in the responsibility for the effectiveness of the care of souls. As the council fathers point out, laypeople bring to the church people who perhaps are far removed from it, help to present the word of God through catechetical instruction and other ways, and "offer their special skills to make the care of souls and the administration of the temporalities of the Church more efficient and effective" (AA 10).

The conciliar phrase *care of souls*, then, was a formal reference to the sacred ministry of the church that was normally restricted to the clergy. As seen above, the council opened the door to increased lay involvement in these pastoral activities. This lay pastoral ministry was not restricted to situations of clergy shortage or persecution, however, as first envisioned by the council. Instead, there was an explosion of lay involvement in the pastoral work of the church in many areas that Vatican II never anticipated. Far from limiting the pastoral ministries of the laity, there seemed to be widespread encouragement for the laity to become active in the inner life of the church after centuries of virtual passivity.

What Counts as Ministry?

The rapid increase in lay involvement in the inner life of the church challenged the traditional theology of sacred ministry. This phenomenon, which was not anticipated by the council fathers, seemingly defied the way the church had always understood the connection between holy orders and sacred ministry. The theological definitions of ministry that had been in place for centuries in Catholic theology were being questioned and debated. If the care of souls could be undertaken by the lay faithful in some cases, how could the strict connection between priesthood and sacred ministry be retained? That is, if the laity can exercise ministry in the church, then how is the role of the clergy to be understood? Soon after Vatican II, the fundamental questions debated by the council fathers concerning the vocation and mission of the laity took on a brand new importance.

Some theologians attempted to craft a new theology of ministry by mining the theology of baptism in the teachings of Vatican II. All the baptized share in the three offices of Christ as priest, prophet, and king. The office of Christ's priesthood had traditionally been a source for understanding sacred ministry in the Body of Christ. But since the council affirmed that the laity also have a distinctive share in Christ's priesthood, perhaps the phenomenon of lay ministry could also be understood in light of this baptismal participation. While lay ministry certainly differs from the ministry of holy orders, it too is a participation in the priestly ministry of Christ and has legitimacy in its own right.

This theological debate concerning ministry after the council was complicated by the fact that many activities in the church were being called "ministries" even if they were not. The care of souls is a very specific kind of activity and never had the sort of expansive application that developed after Vatican II. In the enthusiasm and excitement after the council, it was common for nearly any sort of lay volunteerism to be called a "ministry." This loose use of theological language often led to a misunderstanding of the more technical theology of ministry.

The ongoing attempts to formulate a renewed theology of ministry were hampered when the word *ministry* was applied to such a broad variety of functions and roles in the church. At times it seemed that every good work had to be considered a ministry. In fact, just twenty-plus years after the council, the 1987 Synod of Bishops was critical of this too-indiscriminate use of the word *ministry*. As Pope John Paul II recounted in *Christifideles Laici*, the bishops wanted a clearer and more precisely formulated theology of ministry that took into account the phenomenon of lay ministry, office, and roles rooted in the sacraments of baptism and confirmation while also remaining faithful to the traditional understanding of the priesthood of Christ rooted in holy orders (CFL 23).

The synod's desire for more precise language and a clearer theology should not be understood as an attempt to curtail or restrict the activities of the laity in the inner life of the church. Instead, it is more helpful to realize that the work of the Holy Spirit is always ahead of the formal theology of the church and there is a constant need for theologians to discern these promptings of the Spirit. The new Pentecost released by the Second Vatican Council brought about the unexpected phenomenon of lay ministry and the church's theology needed to catch up with this movement of the Spirit. The scholarly work of defining ministry more precisely is not meant to squelch the Spirit. On the contrary, a clearer theology of ministry can actually help promote the ministries of the baptized in collaboration with the ministries of the ordained.

Toward a Theology of Lay Ministry

Crafting a theology of lay ministry has been an ongoing endeavor since the council. As the practical experience of the church has unfolded, new questions and new challenges have arisen that call for new directions in theological work. This scholarly work has been enhanced by the encouragement and fostering of lay ministry on the part of pastors. As the appreciation for the renewed conciliar theology of baptism and confirmation deepened, the ministries, offices, and roles of the laity that were connected to pastoral ministry but did not require the character of orders became more widely acknowledged (CFL 23).

ST. PAUL AND MINISTRY

The flowering of lay ministries makes the need for a workable theology even more urgent. As mentioned above, the council started this theological process by looking to the experience and teaching of St. Paul. Like many aspects of conciliar teaching on the laity, the insights of St. Paul are foundational, a fact acknowledged in *Lumen Gentium* 33.

St. Paul's theology of the Body of Christ in 1 Corinthians 12 is of great importance for any theology of lay ministry. St. Paul speaks of varieties of charisms, ministries, and activities that all flow from the same God who is Father, Son, and Spirit. In his first list of gifts, services, or works, he mentions healing, miracle working, prophecy, tongues, and interpretation of tongues, which do not seem to require any "office." But later in chapter 12, St. Paul does list certain offices, such as apostle, teacher, and administrator, which seem to be in another category, perhaps requiring some sort of authorization. "And God has appointed in the church first apostles, second prophets, third teachers..." (1 Cor 12:28). This second category seems to be closer to what is understood as ministry today. It must be admitted, however, that St. Paul's terminology is quite fluid when he speaks of ministry or service. At times his descriptions of ministry embrace both "official" and, it might be said, "unofficial" forms of activities all dedicated to the building up of the Body of Christ.

This teaching of St. Paul is also at the foundation of Pope John Paul II's theology of ministry. The pope affirms that "the Apostle Paul is quite clear in speaking about the ministerial constitution of the Church in apostolic times." Referring to St. Paul's teaching on charisms in 1 Corinthians, the pope points out that "these and other New Testament texts indicate the diversity of ministries as well as of gifts and ecclesial tasks" (CFL 21).

St. Paul's discourse in Ephesians 4 on the purpose and use of charisms is also an important consideration in any theology of lay ministry. Reflecting on the reality of baptism, St. Paul claims that the grace of the Holy Spirit is lavished upon the church to bring all to spiritual maturity and full stature in Christ.

> But each of us was given grace according to the measure of Christ's gift....The gifts he gave were that some would be apostles, some prophets, some evangelists, some pastors and teachers, to equip the saints for the work of ministry, for building up the body of Christ, until all of us come to the unity of the faith and of the knowledge of the Son of God, to maturity, to the measure of the full stature of Christ. (Ephesians 4:7, 11–13)

CHURCH AS COMMUNION

This theology of the church as the Body of Christ and the role of charisms in the lives of all believers is perhaps best understood in the context of the theological notion of communion, as explained in chapter two. By presenting the church as a communion, St. Paul highlights the fundamental unity of all of its members. The bond of sharing that unites all the members of the church communion— past, present, and future—is the Holy Spirit. This Spirit gives birth to the diverse vocations, ministries, and roles in the life of the church. The dynamism of the Holy Spirit, as manifested in the charisms given to believers, empowers ministries for the building up of the Body of Christ. Any theology of lay ministry should be based in this theology of communion.

The view of the church as a communion is grounded in the reality of the web of relationships created through baptism.

Through baptism, believers are plunged into a profound communion or relationship with God and with one another. These relationships are not haphazard; they are ordered within the life of the church as a community of believers. The reason why these relationships are ordered is that the church is born from the ordered inner life of the Trinity itself. There is one God in three persons, distinct according to their relationships to each other, yet one in nature. This triune God is a communion of dynamic relationships among the Father, Son, and Holy Spirit. The three persons of God are ordered in that they pour themselves out in eternal love and self-gift in an ordered communion of persons.

The communion of the church, therefore, is to reflect this ordering in its ministerial relationships. The diversity and variety of ministries that complement one another are all united through the Holy Spirit. The various gifts, roles, and ministries in the church are not adversarial; on the contrary, they actually are mutually dependent upon one another and, indeed, enrich one another. Within this theology of communion, distinctions in ministry are necessary and beneficial. These distinctions actually manifest the organic and ordered relationships created through baptism and the presence of charisms within the communion of believers. This communion approach to the life of the church is very helpful in articulating any theology of lay ministry since it avoids the earlier view of the church as an unequal society. The fathers of Vatican II changed this view dramatically by emphasizing instead the church as a communion of believers, equal in dignity and sharing a common mission.

The common mission of the church, as explained in chapter four, is another important component of any theology of lay ministry. Mission flows from communion as is seen in the inner life of the Trinity itself. Within the triune God, the Father sends forth the Word, Jesus, and the Holy Spirit in mission to the world. These missions of the Son and the Spirit are a manifestation of God's love for the world. The church is then called and empowered to fulfill this mission in the world. Baptism plunges all believers into this activity and it is this common mission that must serve as a foundation for any consideration of church ministry.

DISTINCTIONS AND DIFFERENCES

Another important component in articulating a theology of lay ministry is the distinction and differences between ordained and lay ministries. One way of distinguishing these diverse ministries has been to use functionality as a starting point—that is, what laypersons can or cannot do in church ministry. In this line of thinking, the clergy are empowered to perform certain functions that the laity cannot, and it is the performance of those functions that creates the difference between ordained and lay ministries. While attractive on some level, this approach is not actually helpful, since it is nearly impossible to establish a list of functions that have always and everywhere throughout the history of the church been the exclusive preserve of the clergy.

Perhaps a more fruitful way of respecting faithfully the differences between lay and ordained ministries is to explore how both laity and clergy share in the office of the priesthood of Christ, although in distinct ways. As seen above, although all the members of the church participate in the priestly mission of Christ through baptism, there is a distinction in participation that comes from the sacrament of holy orders. Highlighting the differences between the ordained priesthood and the sharing of the priesthood of Christ by the laity, the pope affirms that the ordained ministries embody a participation in the priesthood of Christ that differs both in degree and in essence from the participation conferred on all the lay faithful through baptism and confirmation (CFL 23). At the same time, however, these ordained ministries are ordered to and aim at "the royal priesthood of all the faithful" (CFL 23).

TWO-SPHERE APPROACH?

Even more than forty years after Vatican II, distinguishing between the ministry of the clergy and lay ministry is an ongoing theological endeavor. Focusing only on functions or tasks is not helpful; nor is using the secular character of the lay vocation and mission as a way of distinguishing lay ministry. It would be untrue to claim that the lay faithful are solely responsible for the mission of the church in the world and the clergy are responsible for the inner life and mission of the church. As explained in chapters two and four, the secular character of the laity does not make them "worldly" or keep them from the sacred activities of the mission of the church.

The two-sphere approach of sacred versus secular finds no basis in the teachings of the council. It would be a mistake to assert a hard and fast distinction between the ministry of the laity and that of the clergy that would create two separate spheres for ministry, clergy within the church and laity in the secular realm. After all, the entire church has a secular dimension, and every baptized believer has the responsibility for transforming the world with the values of the Gospel. The whole church "serves as a leaven and as a kind of soul for human society as it is to be renewed in Christ and transformed into God's family" (GS 40).

LAY MINISTRY OR LAY APOSTOLATE?

The two-sphere approach to understanding the mission of the church has led to a certain dichotomizing of church and world in which the inner life of the church is the preserve of the clergy and the world is the only place for the laity. This theological approach is endorsed by some who think that there has been too much emphasis on the rapidly expanding lay ministries in the church, which obscures the proper secular mission of the laity. Unfortunately, this attitude results in a highly clericalized church and a laity reduced to second-class citizenship in the inner life and mission of the church.

By dividing the secular and sacred realms in this way, the language of service is also altered to match these divisions. There is a tendency to reserve the use of the terms *ministry* and *ministers* only for the ordained and never apply them to the laity. *Ministry*, it is argued, should only be used as a designation for established offices in the church, held by the clergy. The activities of the laity should be called an "apostolate," not a ministry. *Apostolate* refers to activities directed outward to the world, the proper secular realm for any lay involvement.

This dichotomy in language between "apostolate" and "ministry" seems to be driven by the concern that stressing lay ministry within the church would undermine any lay activities directed toward the world. Somehow it is feared that the secular character of the laity is being downplayed or forgotten if lay ministry is promoted in church teaching or practice. Those who support the two-realm approach to the church's mission contend that a focus on lay ministry devalues the responsibility of the laity to transform political, social, and economic institutions in the world.

The two-realm approach of clerical "ministry" versus lay "apostolate" does not, however, seem to be warranted by the council's teaching, still less by Scripture and tradition. The entire church has "an authentic secular dimension inherent to her inner nature and mission, which is deeply rooted in the mystery of the Word Incarnate, and which is realized in different forms through her members" (CFL 15). Every member of the church lives in the world, even if not "of the world" (John 17:16), and shares the responsibility "to continue the redemptive work of Jesus Christ, which, by its very nature concerns the salvation of humanity, and also involves the renewal of the whole temporal order" (CFL 15).

Any sharp dichotomy between ministry in the church and apostolate in the world would give the mistaken impression that it is necessary to choose between the two. Lay ministry that edifies and builds up the life of the church can strengthen any service directed to the transformation of the world. By sharing in the building up of communion in the church, lay ministries can empower all members of the church to live the Gospel witness in the world. Far from devaluing lay service in the world, lay ministries can actually provide formation and spiritual guidance for these secular works and initiatives. Lay ministry is not a distraction from the secular character of the vocation and mission of the laity; instead, it can be the means by which lay, clergy, and religious are formed, trained, and sent into the world for the sake of the redemptive mission of Christ.

Co-Workers in the Vineyard of the Lord

One important contribution to the ongoing development of a theology of lay ecclesial ministry was the publication in 2005 of

Co-Workers in the Vineyard of the Lord by the United States Conference of Catholic Bishops. Subtitled *A Resource for Guiding the Development of Lay Ecclesial Ministry* and not intended to set down norms, it is a resource for bishops who wish to use it. *Co-Workers* relates a brief history of lay ecclesial ministry in the United States, offers models of training, and provides an overview for a theological foundation of this postconciliar reality.

Co-Workers is an excellent example of the ongoing work of appropriating the Second Vatican Council's teaching on the laity while adapting it to address new pastoral situations and phenomena. The Holy Spirit seems to be continuing to lead the church in rediscovering the reality of its own inner life and mission as found in the New Testament. This is what happened at Vatican II and is still happening in the church today, as is evidenced by the publication of *Co-Workers* in 2005. It is a landmark document in that there is no other magisterial document on the topic of ministry like it that integrates ordained and lay ministries. No other bishops' conference around the world has provided such a resource that combines a theology of emerging ministries with the Second Vatican Council's theology of the church.

The result of ten years of consultations between bishops and lay ecclesial ministers, *Co-Workers* pushes the conversation about ministry forward in its clear articulations of practical topics such as training models and formation goals as well as theological topics such as communion and mission. The U.S. bishops recognize that lay ecclesial ministry is a reality that continues to unfold and develop, and yet they are committed to the ongoing task of crafting a theology that matches this praxis. *Co-Workers* is not the final word on the matter, nor is it even a legal mandate of church norms or law for lay ecclesial ministry. Instead, it is meant to provide a theological and pastoral framework so that lay ecclesial ministry continues to develop in ways faithful to the church's theological and doctrinal tradition and that respond to contemporary pastoral needs and situations.[3]

The structure of the document itself shows how any consideration of lay ecclesial ministry must be grounded in a theology of the church and ministry before it can address more practical concerns of policies and praxis.

STRUCTURE OF THE DOCUMENT

The boldness of the bishops' document is reflected in its call for a renewal in ministry. This renewal will occur when lay ecclesial ministers are properly understood and effectively integrated into the church's life. Of course, it must be admitted that this renewal is a process that can be, at times, uneven across the United States, sometimes slow, and usually progressing by fits and starts. As the bishops themselves admit, "The Church's experience of lay participation in Christ's ministry is still maturing" (*Co-Workers*, 15).

In an effort to understand properly who they are, the bishops recognize lay ecclesial ministers as a distinct group. It is *lay* ministry because it is founded on the sacraments of initiation rather than the sacrament of Holy Orders. It is *ecclesial* because it is approved and supervised by church authority and because it aims at building up the church. And it is truly a *ministry* because it is a participation in the threefold ministry of Christ as priest, prophet, and king.

Part one of the document affirms and legitimizes lay ecclesial ministry by demonstrating its theological foundations. The bishops employ the theology of communion and mission rooted in the trinitarian mystery and reflected in the church. Here they are relying on the theology of Vatican II and Pope John Paul II's *Christifideles Laici*. Part two outlines a serious formation for lay ecclesial ministry. The bishops mention human, spiritual, intellectual, and pastoral formation. This section also makes suggestions for institutionalizing and integrating lay ecclesial ministry within the life of the whole church. This includes authorization by the local bishop.

SELECT THEOLOGICAL THEMES

Some of the most important theological themes in *Co-Workers* include: vocation, sacramental identity, communion, charisms, secular character, and ministry. The bishops maintain that the theology of the document must guide any implementation of it. "Our understanding, assessment, and action must be contextualized theologically and expressed in faithfulness to the Church's belief and teaching" (*Co-Workers*, 17).

Vocation

The first theological theme is the idea of the call or vocation of the laity. God calls everyone to relationship with him, and this call is also a vocation to holiness. The bishops begin with Vatican II's "universal call to holiness" from *Lumen Gentium* 40 "that all Christians in whatever state or walk of life are called to the fullness of Christian life and to the perfection of charity, and this holiness is conducive to a more human way of living even in society here on earth" (*Co-Workers*, 7). This universal call to holiness is presented by the bishops as being at the very root of lay ecclesial ministry. Later in the document the bishops make an explicit link between the gift of holiness, or union with God in charity, and the responsibility for mission, so that this gift becomes a mission that must shape the whole of the Christian life (*Co-Workers*, 19).

Sacramental Basis

The bishops ground the realities of mission and ministry in the sacraments. The sacramental identity of the laity is their foundation for ministry. What is interesting is that *Co-Workers* considers matrimony as a "mission sacrament" along with baptism and confirmation (*Co-Workers*, 9). Here the bishops are following the lead of Vatican II in *Apostolicam Actuositatem* 10.

Communion

Co-Workers understands lay ministry as based in the theology of communion, a theology rooted in the inner life of the Trinity itself and defined by the dynamic relationships among the Father, Son, and Holy Spirit. This communion of relationships, or *communio*, is one God in three persons, distinct according to their relationships to each other, yet one in nature. "The one true God is fundamentally relational: a loving communion of persons, Father, Son, and Holy Spirit. The mystery of God is one of love, the love of Trinitarian communion revealed in mission" (*Co-Workers*, 17).

Baptism is the believer's entrance into this communion, uniting all members of the church in a profound way with God and one another. The church is itself, then, a communion, one in Christ, and one in his mission of announcing the Kingdom of God and transforming the world with the power of the Holy Spirit. "The Church finds its source and purpose in the life and activity of the Triune God" (*Co-Workers*, 19). The bishops use Pope John Paul II's description of the church as a "mystery of Trinitarian communion in missionary tension" to link *communio* and mission (*Co-Workers*, 19).

From this foundation of communion, diverse charisms, roles, and functions are not in competition, but rather are complementary within the mission of the church. Every gift and manifestation of the Spirit is given for the building up of the Body of Christ. It is within this communion ecclesiology that *Co-Workers* understands distinctions in ministry, seeing them as necessary and pointing out how they "illuminate the nature of the Church as an organic and ordered communion" (*Co-Workers*, 20).

These distinctions are not a ranking of importance or of merit or holiness. Rather, distinctions in ministry, based on an ecclesiology of communion, can reveal the nature of the church itself, which is an organic and ordered communion made up of diverse parts. It is precisely this communion that makes possible and necessary the collaboration between lay and ordained ministers.

Charisms

The gifts of the Holy Spirit are poured out in baptism and confirmation and are directed toward the building up of the whole church. The theological component of charisms in this document is based on *Lumen Gentium* 12, which states that charisms are ordered "to the building up of the Church, to the well-being of humanity, and to the needs of the world." *Co-Workers* calls for charisms to be "tested and guided by the Church's pastors, with the assistance of spiritual directors, formation directors, mentors, and others" so that they might be coordinated for the edification of the whole Body of Christ (*Co-Workers*, 18–19). Charisms manifest a diversity of ministry within a unity of mission in the Church (*Co-Workers*, 19).

Secular Character

The secular character of the laity refers to the fact that lay men and women hear and answer the call to holiness uniquely and primarily in their everyday lives. Reflecting on the teaching of Vatican II, the bishops affirm that secular character acknowledges that the lay faithful live, work, play, and raise families in this context and act as a leaven to sanctify the world from within. *Co-Workers* certainly does not create a two-realm approach to ministry based on secular character, however. Instead, it raises the question of how this secular character might be expressed in the building up of the communion of the inner life of the church itself. Lay ecclesial ministers express their secular character uniquely not by working in the secular realm, but "by working in the Church and focusing on the building of ecclesial communion, which has among its purposes the transformation of the world. Working in the Church is a path of Christian discipleship to be encouraged by the hierarchy" (*Co-Workers*, 8).

Ministry

The last theological theme of *Co-Workers* that will be mentioned is the concept of ministry itself, described by the bishops as "service (*diakonia*)," which is "the means for accomplishing mission in the communion of the Church" and a "participation in and expression of Christ's ministry. Within this broad understanding of ministry, distinctions are necessary. They illuminate the nature of the Church as an organic and ordered communion" (*Co-Workers*, 20). This description of ministry in the bishops' document does not restrict it to the clergy but rather opens it up to a broader understanding that better reflects the praxis in the United States over the past forty years.

The bishops' approach to ministry is relational in that it emphasizes roles that are different but that complement one another in the communion of the church. "An ecclesiology of communion looks upon different gifts and functions not as adversarial but as enriching and complementary" (*Co-Workers*, 20). The church is an ordered communion with a great diversity of ministries and Christian activities that together build up the life of the church. The ordering of ministerial relationships reflects the ordered inner life of the Trinity itself. The triune God is a communion of dynamic relationships of self-giving love among the Father, Son, and Holy Spirit. The diversity of ministries is best articulated, it seems, through this theology of communion that stresses unity within the diversity of ordered sacramental relationships. "The further development and ordering of right relationships among those called to public ministries is done with a view to enabling all the disciples to realize their calling to holiness and service. By examining these relationships we can arrive at a better appreciation of the specific place of lay ecclesial ministers in an ordered, relational, ministerial community" (*Co-Workers*, 21).

Co-Workers in the Vineyard of the Lord is a response from the U.S. Catholic Bishops to new realities present in the church's life and ministries. It offers theological and pastoral resources to dioceses, programs, and academic institutions for the recognition of lay ecclesial ministry within the context of a broader renewal in how ecclesial lay and ordained ministries are understood and organized. It is truly a ground-breaking document because it attempts to formulate a theology of lay ministry based on the lived experience of the church in the United States since the Second Vatican Council.

Conclusion

During the deliberations of the Second Vatican Council, lay ecclesial ministry in the church was truly an unforeseen grace of the Holy Spirit. Although unexpected by the council fathers, it has been an integral part of the ongoing renewal of the church in the past forty years. The praxis of lay men and women exercising roles traditionally reserved for the clergy has developed at a faster pace than any formal theology, however. Therefore, it is necessary for the church to reflect on this phenomenon and articulate a theology that is faithful to Scripture and tradition, and yet open to new movements of the Spirit.

In the ongoing development of the theology of lay ecclesial ministry, it is important to resist the tendency to have everything clear, cut and dried, and neatly categorized. To hasten the process unnecessarily would risk blocking developments that have not yet reached the point of maturity. It is vital that patient and persevering discernment is fostered among all the members of the church, clergy and lay, as a way of following the Spirit's lead. As the years since Vatican II have demonstrated, times of change are difficult and bring with them inevitable tensions and challenges. Certainly, clarity about the church's faith needs to be combined with a spirit of humility and charity. Whatever the outcome of the continuing grappling with the questions of ministry, what should always be promoted and deepened is the communion of the church, which is the only true source of mission.

Reflection Questions

1. What was St. Paul's experience and theology of ministry in the church?

2. Explain how the "care of souls" is distinct from simple volunteer work in the church.

3. How have you witnessed the shifts in ministry in your own parish?

4. What are the tensions inherent in any theology of lay ministry?

5. Has your diocese used any of the resources in the bishops' document *Co-Workers in the Vineyard of the Lord*?

CHAPTER SIX

The Spirituality of the Laity

Genuinely Lay Spirituality

The universal call to holiness issued by the Second Vatican Council put an end to any notion that the laity were somehow exempt from the hard work of Christian discipleship. Clergy and religious were no longer seen to have an advantage over the laity when it came to spiritual growth. The council's call for the lay faithful to completely embrace their baptismal identity was at the same time a challenge to reconsider holiness not as an impossible ideal, but rather as a Gospel imperative. Christ made no distinctions in his call to his followers to "Be perfect, therefore, as your heavenly Father is perfect" (Matt 5:48). As explained in chapter three, the council's teaching on holiness raised expectations and affirmed the reality of a genuinely lay spirituality: "...all the faithful, whatever their condition or state, are called by the Lord, each in his own way, to that perfect holiness whereby the Father Himself is perfect" (LG 11).

The lay condition or state was not to be considered an obstacle or hindrance to true growth in holiness. Spiritual progress was not encumbered by the layperson's life in the world. On the contrary, the secular character of the lay vocation and mission should be embraced as a grace that shapes how laypeople answer the call to sanctity. The council's emphasis on the spiritual value of daily life made it possible for the laity to see their daily activities, struggles, triumphs, and hopes as opportunities to grow in holiness and union with God.

A genuinely lay spirituality takes seriously the genuine human experiences and daily existence of the lay life. Relationships, encounters, situations, and events take on a whole new meaning when seen through the lens of faith. Lay spirituality should be suited to the lay life in the world and should account for the circumstances people face each day. It would be fruitless to attempt to impose a "pseudo-clerical" or "pseudo-religious" spirituality onto the laity. Not only would this be impractical; more importantly, it would contradict the council's teaching concerning the dignity and importance of the secular character of the lay faithful. As *Lumen Gentium* points out, the laity bring glory to God by living out their secular character (LG 31).

Only by fashioning a spiritual life according to the contours of family life, work, and friendships will lay men and women be pointed toward the world in order to permeate the workplace, school, home, or neighborhood with the values of the Gospel. The council sought to emphasize that things like family life and secular concerns are the very stuff of holiness in the lives of the laity. Virtually nothing in the lives of laypersons is peripheral to their spirituality. The council fathers recognize that the lay faithful live in the world, in each and in all of the secular professions and occupations, and that they "are called there by God" (LG 31).

Pope John Paul II also taught that all aspects of daily life must be integrated into lay spirituality. These include "skill and solidarity in work, love and dedication in the family and the education of children, service to society and public life and the promotion of truth in the area of culture" (CFL 59).

Lay Spirituality in the Teaching of Vatican II

Although it issued a universal call to holiness and highlighted the secular character of the laity, it must be admitted that the council did not actually formulate a lay spirituality. This lack of a full-blown lay spirituality in the documents of the council is significant. It shows that a genuinely lay spirituality must be crafted by lay men and women themselves. They are to be the ones who create a spirituality that suits their lives in the world. And so while the council did offer some principles and perspectives on the spiritual lives of laypeople, it left the door open for them to formulate their own response to the call to holiness.

In its broadest sense, spirituality simply means living out one's faith and becoming increasingly more aware of the incorporation into Christ that comes through baptism. Spirituality is a lifelong process of growth into the sanctification and holiness that are the goal of the Christian life. This growth is a conscious experience of union with Christ through prayer and a life lived in conformity with his teachings (LG 40).

For the laity, spirituality means to formulate an understanding of holiness that raises awareness of God's presence in the world and in their ordinary lives. Christian maturity for laypeople, then, includes witnessing to Christ in temporal affairs according to their state in life and personal gifts and talents. And through their holiness, the council fathers maintained, laypersons act as a leaven for society. All faithful Christians, regardless of status, "are called to the fullness of the Christian life and to the perfection of charity; by this holiness as such a more human manner of living is promoted in this earthly society" (LG 40).

Priest, Prophet, and King

By their baptism, the laity share in the threefold offices of Christ as priest, prophet, and king. In its teachings on how laypeople, in particular, live out these three offices, the council offers a few insights concerning lay spirituality. Shaped by their sacramental identity and their secular character, the lay faithful have a distinctive sharing in the sanctifying, prophetic, and royal dimensions of Christ's mission. And each of these offices informs the call to holiness of the laity.

The lay faithful share in the priestly office of the One who offered himself as the ultimate sacrifice on the altar of the cross for the salvation of the world. As priest, Christ offers the once and for all sacrifice that brings about the redemption of the whole human race. All the baptized share in the responsibility to offer this redemption to all and thereby to further Christ's saving work. In a special way, the laity engage the priestly dimension of their vocation and mission by their "liturgy of daily life." None of the individual struggles or situations of their everyday lives falls outside of the scope of their participation in Christ's loving and redeeming self-sacrifice; they all have the potential to become "spiritual sacrifices acceptable to God through Jesus Christ" (LG 34).

The laity also share in the prophetic office of the One who is the Word made flesh. Christ is the final revelation of the Father and brings the definitive word of salvation which is God's love and life for the world. Through word and deed, Christ is the greatest prophet who ushers in the kingdom of God. The lay faithful are called to be powerful and courageous witnesses of this word in temporal activities as they act as salt, light, and leaven for the world. The power of the Gospel must shine out in daily family and social life, "in the ordinary surroundings of the world" (LG 35).

The laity share in the kingly or royal office of the One who is king of kings and ruler of the cosmos. By his death and resurrection, Christ is revealed as the sovereign over life and death. In the glory of his kingdom, all things are subject to him. All the baptized are to share in spreading this kingdom and ordering all of creation under its saving power. The kingship of Christ is realized when sin is overcome and the church's mission of justice, peace, and love is accomplished. Here the council stresses that the reality of work also shapes laypeople's call to holiness since their daily labors are a sharing in Christ's kingly office: they contribute their efforts "so that created goods may be perfected by human labor, technical skill and civic culture for the benefit of all men according to the design of the Creator and the light of His Word" (LG 36).

Some Basic Components

The Second Vatican Council provided some basic components for crafting a spirituality of the laity flowing from these three offices of priest, prophet, and king. It must be admitted, however, that these basic components are not exclusive to lay spirituality; indeed, all members of the church should incorporate them into their Christian journey of holiness. But the manner in which these components will be configured in the life of an individual will depend largely on the layperson's state of life and circumstances. One size does not fit all when it comes to Christian spirituality. Therefore, the wisdom of the council's teaching is that these spiritual resources will be lived out in a diversity of ways by the laity, clergy, and religious. "Every person must walk unhesitatingly according to his own personal gifts and duties in the path of living faith, which arouses hope and works through charity" (LG 41).

The Christian life is a relationship with Christ lived out on a daily basis. This union with Christ gives meaning, shape, and purpose to the life of any member of the church. Here there is really no distinction among lay, clergy, and religious; all are incorporated into Christ through baptism and are set on a journey of faith that unfolds as one grows in this relationship with God and others. Therefore, the most basic and fundamental reality in any spirituality is union with Christ, which then, in turn, flows into mission in a variety of ways.

> ...the success of the lay apostolate depends upon the laity's living union with Christ, in keeping with the Lord's words, "He who abides in me, and I in him, bears much fruit, for without me you can do nothing" (John 15:5). This life of intimate union with Christ in the Church is nourished by spiritual aids which are common to all the faithful.... (AA 4)

WORD OF GOD

The first spiritual help common to all the faithful that the council highlights is the Word of God. The Scriptures are an indispensable source of nourishment for the Christian life. Divinely inspired through the Holy Spirit, the Bible is the living Word of God spoken to every believer and to the church as a whole. Far from a dead letter, the scriptures are a living challenge and invitation to relationship with God. As St. Paul urges: "Let the word of Christ dwell in you richly; teach and admonish one another in all wisdom..." (Col 3:16). It is through this indwelling of the Word of God that relationship with God grows.

The council fathers encourage the laity to make the Word of God an integral part of their spiritual lives. Certainly, the Word is proclaimed in the Mass and other liturgical celebrations, but laypeople are also urged to read the Bible privately. Earlier, the church hesitated to allow the laity to read the Bible on their own, for fear of erroneous private interpretations that might contradict its teachings. But Vatican II changed this attitude in its directives to the lay faithful to make the scriptures a basic component of their spirituality. "Indeed, in order that love, as good seed may grow and bring forth fruit in the soul, each one of the faithful must willingly hear the Word of God and accept His Will, and must complete what God has begun by their own actions with the help of God's grace" (LG 42). This exhortation has led to a renewal in Bible studies, parish courses, and publications specifically directed toward laypeople for their spiritual growth.

Laypeople need the guidance and inspiration of the Bible to enable them to discover God's will and to judge rightly the things of this world. As the council fathers state:

> Only by the light of faith and by meditation on the word of God can one always and everywhere recognize God in Whom "we live, and move, and have our being" (Acts 17:28), seek His will in every event...and make correct judgments about the true meaning and value of temporal things.... (AA 4)

SACRAMENTS

Being grounded in the Word of God is to be complemented with participation in the sacramental life of the church. The sacraments are another fundamental component to the spirituality of the laity. The Holy Spirit is both the soul of the Body of Christ, the church, and the source for its sacramental life. The sacraments are not mere human ceremonies, family rituals, or rites of passage. They are ways of actually encountering God during the journey of faith. These direct sacramental encounters with God nourish and strengthen believers in living out their vocation and mission in the church and in the world. The sacraments are unique ways of communicating God's presence and power. The sacraments are to heal, transform, and shape the lives of laypeople as they grow in holiness.

The heart of the sacramental life is the Eucharist, since it is the very body and blood of Christ himself. Therefore, the council singles out the Eucharist and participation in the liturgy as fundamental for lay spirituality (LG 42; see also AA 3). The liturgy, the worship life of the church, should inform the lives of laypeople on every level. The healing graces of the Eucharist and the spiritual dynamism of the liturgy nourish the lay faithful in their relationships with God and others. "This life of intimate union with Christ in the church is nourished by spiritual aids which are common to all the faithful, especially active participation in the sacred liturgy" (AA 4).

Vatican II attempted to move the laity away from the attitude that Mass is a weekly "obligation" to the knowledge that the liturgy and reception of the Eucharist is rather a weekly "celebration" and encounter with the risen Lord. Indeed, the renewal in liturgical life since the council has invited the lay faithful to a more active participation in the sacramental life of the church, especially the Mass and Eucharist.

PRAYER

The Christian life cannot exist without prayer. Prayer is the communication with God that undergirds all of the components of the spiritual life. The life and ministry of Christ himself had prayer as a foundation. The Gospels bear out this importance of prayer in the life of Christ. He prayed to his Father in the power of the Holy Spirit at many points of his life. Whenever he healed the sick, freed the demonically possessed, or raised the dead, he did it with prayer. As he faced arrest in Gethsemane or hung from the cross on Golgotha, Jesus prayed to the Father in the communion of the Holy Spirit. And Christ instructed his followers to plunge themselves into a life of prayer. "When you are praying, do not heap up empty phrases as the Gentiles do; for they think that they will be heard because of their many words. Do not be like them, for your Father knows what you need before you ask him. Pray then in this way: Our Father in heaven, hallowed be your name..." (Matt 6:7–9).

Traditionally, a common misconception was that a life steeped in prayer was the prerogative only of those who chose the monastic or ascetical vocations: religious men and women seemed to be the "professional pray-ers." The expectations for lay spirituality were therefore quite low as it was thought that laypersons' lives in the world precluded them from serious prayer and contemplation. The monastic life, after all, even organized the hours in the day around prayer. But laypersons did not have this "luxury," since their lives were organized instead around family cares and work obligations. It was thought that the prayer lives of lay men and women were diminished at best.

But the Second Vatican Council raised the expectations for lay spirituality by saying that the lay faithful must "constantly apply themselves to prayer" (LG 42). How, indeed, were the laity to address the exhortation of St. Paul to "pray without ceasing" (1 Thess 5:17)? The council affirmed that the lay faithful were called to a life informed by prayer that took seriously their temporal concerns and secular occupations. Instead of ascetical prayer schedules or monastic vows of silence, laypersons are to encounter God and communicate with him right in the midst of daily life.

The messiness of the mundane is where the laity are challenged to offer up their prayers, cries, and supplications to God who sees, hears, and knows all. The busy lives of laypeople offer many occasions for conversation with God. The constant stream of people and situations encountered can give their prayer a unique texture and richness. Far from being obstacles to prayer, these occasions are the very conditions under which ordinary Catholics can grow in union with God (AA 4).

CHARISMS AND VIRTUES

Through baptism, every believer receives the Holy Spirit. Confirmation is a fuller, deeper release of the Holy Spirit in power. Christ promised the indwelling presence of the Holy Spirit as a lasting gift to his followers. After the ascension, Christians would not be orphaned, but would experience God's presence in an intimate way through the Holy Spirit dwelling within their hearts. "And I will ask the Father, and he will give you another Advocate, to be with you forever. This is the Spirit of truth, whom the world cannot receive, because it neither sees him nor knows him. You know him, because he abides with you, and he will be in you. I will not leave you orphaned; I am coming to you" (John 14:16–18).

Pope John XXIII prayed that the Second Vatican Council would be a new Pentecost that would renew the church. And the teachings of the council do indeed reflect this emphasis on the power and activity of the Holy Spirit in the church: "From the acceptance of these charisms, including those which are more elementary, there arise for each believer the right and duty to use them in the Church and in the world for the good of men and the building up of the Church..." (AA 3).

In speaking of the laity's call to discipleship and their spiritual lives, this charismatic emphasis is significant. The gifts or charisms given through the outpouring of the Holy Spirit are not limited to the clergy and religious; laypeople also receive the Holy Spirit's graces and energy to follow the call of Christ to love and service. These charisms given by the Holy Spirit are another resource for the spirituality of the lay faithful.

> This plan for the spiritual life of the laity should take its particular character from their married or family state or their single or widowed state, from their state of health, and from their professional and social activity. They should not cease to develop earnestly the qualities and talents bestowed on them in accord with these conditions of life, and they should make use of the gifts which they have received from the Holy Spirit. (AA 4)

Besides the charisms of the Holy Spirit, the theological virtues of faith, hope, and charity are also an important component for lay spirituality since through them the Christian life of love and service is made possible. These virtues are bestowed through baptism and unfold as the Christian journey progresses. A life of holiness is one marked in a special way by the manifestation of these three virtues in action. According to the council, the life of the laity in the midst of the world is a particular challenge to live and witness to these three virtues.

In this way the laity must make progress in holiness in
a happy and ready spirit, trying prudently and patiently
to overcome difficulties....Such a life requires a continual exercise of faith, hope, and charity. (AA 4)

Faith, hope, and charity are mutually dependent upon one
another. That is, the deepening of one of the virtues affects the
other two. Faith is the beginning of the Christian life. And as faith
grows, it gives rise to Christian hope based on the resurrection victory of Christ over sin and death. This Christian hope, based on
the resurrection, then motivates the believer for a life of charity
toward others. "Every person must walk unhesitatingly according
to his own personal gifts and duties in the path of living faith,
which arouses hope and works through charity" (LG 41).

FAMILY, FRIENDSHIPS, AND ASSOCIATIONS

The Christian life is lived out in communion with God and
others. Therefore, another important component in lay spirituality is relationships with others. In addition to the Word of God,
sacraments, prayer, liturgical life, charisms, and virtues, the
council also highlights relationships with other believers as a
resource for the spiritual lives of the lay faithful. Relationships
with others can be a critical source of edification as men and
women seek the support and witness of Christian holiness in
daily life. As St. Paul exhorts: "Therefore encourage one another
and build up each other, as indeed you are doing" (1 Thess 5:11).

The importance of family life is first and foremost in the
teaching of the council regarding relationships and lay spirituality. The joys and sorrows, the blessings and challenges of family
life shape the spirituality of the laity in a profound way. Nothing,
whether family concerns or other secular matters, should be irrel-
evant to the spiritual lives of the lay faithful (AA 4). The web of
relationships in marriage and family life presents many opportunities for growing in holiness through a life of charity. The
Christian family is the "church in miniature" and in many ways
the primary school of faith, hope, and love. Christ himself was
part of a family, and the hidden years in Nazareth with Joseph
and Mary can become a model for this aspect of lay spirituality.

Furthermore, married couples and Christian parents should follow their own proper path [to holiness] by faithful love. They should sustain one another in grace throughout the entire length of their lives. They should embue their offspring, lovingly welcomed as God's gift, with Christian doctrine and the evangelical virtues. In this manner, they offer all men the example of unwearying and generous love; in this way they build up the brotherhood of charity; in so doing, they stand as the witnesses and cooperators in the fruitfulness of Holy Mother Church....A like example, but one given in a different way, is that offered by widows and single people, who are able to make great contributions toward holiness and apostolic endeavor in the Church. (LG 41)

In its treatment of family life as a basic factor in lay spirituality, the council links it to the prophetic office of Christ. As mentioned above, the laity's sharing in the three offices of Christ as priest, prophet, and king is a fundamental source for Vatican II's understanding of the vocation, mission, and spirituality of the laity. Here the daily life of the family is presented as a sharing in Christ's prophetic role of proclaiming the kingdom of God through his words and deeds. The lay faithful are called to be witnesses "so that the power of the Gospel might shine forth in their daily social and family life" (LG 35). Vatican II joins together both the vocation and mission of married life within its reflection on the prophetic role of the laity in the world.

In connection with the prophetic function, that state of life which is sanctified by a special sacrament obviously of great importance, namely, married and family life....In such a home husbands and wives find their proper vocation in being witnesses of the faith and love of Christ to one another and to their children. The Christian family loudly proclaims both the present virtues of the Kingdom of God and the hope of a blessed life to come. (LG 35)

The spirituality of the laity is, therefore, profoundly shaped by living through the day-to-day challenges, surprises, and struggles of family life. These relationships are not incidental to laypersons' lives; rather, in a very profound way, it is these relationships that mark out the contours of lay spirituality. The council moves away from the traditional notion that marriage and living in the world were somehow a "concession to human weakness," spiritually inferior to the vowed religious vocations. Instead, the language of the council gives a very exalted view of marriage and family life that is an ecclesial vocation with a mission to transform the world for the sake of Christ.

> This mission—to be the first and vital cell of society—the family has received from God. It will fulfill this mission if it appears as the domestic sanctuary of the Church by reason of the mutual affection of its members and the prayer that they offer to God in common, if the whole family makes itself a part of the liturgical worship of the Church, and if it provides active hospitality and promotes justice and other good works for the service of all the brethren in need....Christian families can give effective testimony to Christ before the world by remaining faithful to the Gospel and by providing a model of Christian marriage through their whole way of life. (AA 11)

After family life, the next level of relationships mentioned by the council is Christian friendship, another critical element in lay spirituality. Having companions on the pilgrimage of faith can be a tremendous source of consolation and encouragement. In fostering Christian friendship, laypeople help one another in every need (AA 4). In fact, Christ himself uses the reality of friendship as a model for Christian community. He calls his disciples "friends" and in so doing gives a spiritual dimension to the human institution of friendship. "No one has greater love than this, to lay down one's life for one's friends. You are my friends if you do what I command you....I have called you friends, because I have made known to you everything that I have heard from my Father" (John

15:13–15). Indeed, friendship with God and Christian friendship with others are an important part of the web of relationships that define lay spirituality.

The final level of relationships identified by the council is lay associations and institutions in the church. Prior to Vatican II, lay sodalities, third orders of religious communities, and Catholic charitable and social institutions were quite popular among lay men and women. These institutions were part of the very fabric of the Catholic subculture in many areas of the church. Typically, these organizations were founded, organized, and controlled by the clergy or religious communities. However, Vatican II encouraged lay autonomy and freedom in forming Christian associations on their own initiative. Since the council, there has been a flowering of lay movements, institutions, and associations within the church that are part of the new Pentecost of lay spirituality. Laypeople who belong to one of the church-approved associations or institutes accept the call to adopt the special characteristics of the spirituality proper to that association (AA 4).

These institutions, movements, and renewal associations with a specifically lay identity usually have distinctive charisms and ministries. The charisms of the founders of these movements typically result in unique spiritualities and traditions that fuel the movement for mission. The life of the church is enhanced when these distinctive charisms and movements can be lived out in harmony in one another. The danger is always in competitiveness or suspicion among these lay associations. The model of engagement for these various movements should be one of complementarity, not competition. The mission of the church flourishes when these distinctive spiritualities and institutions can offer complementary ways of living the lay vocation and mission.

WORK

Another building block for lay spirituality is the experience of labor or work. This component is somewhat surprising, given the traditional popular misconception of the reality of work. A certain reading of the Genesis 3 narrative led to a negative perception of work as Adam's punishment for original sin. God tells

Adam that because he ate the forbidden fruit, he must now work. According to this reading, the human experience of work only became a reality after the Fall into sin by Adam and Eve.

> Cursed is the ground because of you; in toil you shall eat of it all the days of your life; thorns and thistles it shall bring forth for you....By the sweat of your face you shall eat bread until you return to the ground, for out of it you were taken.... (Gen 3:17–19)

Therefore, the popular traditional view of work, taken from this passage in Genesis, was that it was a curse from God. Work was also considered a source of temptations to commit personal sins. The explanation of work in the teachings of Vatican II reversed this misconception, however, by restoring the perception of work as an activity that was a sharing in the very creative powers of God and a participation in Christ's redemption. Humans are cocreators with God, not only by procreation but by work as well. Work is neither a distraction nor a curse; instead, it contributes to the spiritual life of the laity and helps them to grow in holiness.

The teachings of the council fathers connect the office of Christ as king with the reality of work. The lay faithful participate in this royal or kingly office of Christ by valuing and ordering creation according to the plan of God. A concrete expression of the ordering of creation is work. Worldly tasks, daily labors and responsibilities all contribute to the spreading of the kingdom of God and its saving power. A significant part of lay spirituality, then, is an ongoing reflection upon the meaning and value of work.

> They must assist each other to live holier lives even in their daily occupations....Therefore, by their competence in secular training and by their activity, elevated from within by the grace of Christ, let them vigorously contribute their effort, so that created goods may be perfected by human labor, technical skill and civic culture for the benefit of all men according to the design of the Creator and the light of His Word. (LG 36)

The council points to the example of Christ himself, who, by tradition, worked as a carpenter. The lay faithful are called to imitate Christ, who used carpenter's tools and, in union with his Father, works continually for the salvation of all (LG 41). Christ's human labor becomes a model and source of reflection for lay men and women as they engage in various forms of work.

By considering human work through the context of the kingly office of Christ, the lay faithful can more easily see labor as a means for ushering in the kingdom of God. Work is not to be considered as a source of temptation, but rather as an opportunity for holiness in daily life. Work can be a means of sanctifying the individual and transforming the world for God whereby laypeople "climb to the heights of holiness and apostolic activity" (LG 41).

SUFFERING

The final building block for the spirituality of the laity that will be discussed here is the role of suffering in the Christian life. Suffering, which has many levels and dimensions, can often be the most challenging aspect of the life of a disciple of Christ. From the penetrating questions of the suffering Job in the Old Testament to the struggles with the apparent meaninglessness of much suffering in the world today, believers have always had to contend with this deep mystery. Vatican II urged the laity to consider suffering—whether poverty, sickness, persecution, or other hardships—through the lens of the sufferings of Christ himself (LG 41).

One of the deepest mysteries of the Christian faith is that God himself suffered in Christ and by that suffering brought about the redemption of all. "Although he was a Son, he learned obedience through what he suffered; and having been made perfect, he became the source of eternal salvation for all who obey him..." (Heb 5:8–9). Even the apostles struggled with this reality and had to be enlightened by the risen Lord as to the purpose of his shameful death. He asks the two disciples on the road to Emmaus: "Was it not necessary that the Messiah should suffer these things and then enter into his glory?" (Luke 24:26). Indeed, it is only in the light of the resurrection that the mystery of the sufferings of Christ can take on any meaning.

The teaching of the council makes a link between the sufferings of Christ and the sufferings of his followers through the priestly office. This baptismal sharing in the priestly office of Christ is the key to their understanding of how suffering is part of the Christian life. The challenge of integrating the experience of suffering into the life of faith can be met only if the lay faithful remember the sufferings of Christ in his role as both priest and victim on the cross. His self-sacrificing death as an innocent victim is the suffering that saves the whole human race. By sharing in this priestly office, the laity are able to join their sufferings with those of Christ and participate in the redemption of the world.

It should be stressed that this spiritual offering of sufferings great and small does not lessen their severity or pain. The priestly office does not take away suffering from the laity; instead, it is a way of spiritually integrating suffering into the ups and downs, the joys and sorrows of the pilgrimage of faith. By considering the whole Christian life as a means of spiritual sacrifice, the priestly office can at least give a framework for this integration of suffering in lay spirituality. This framework is offered by St. Peter when he urges: "...like living stones, let yourselves be built into a spiritual house, to be a holy priesthood, to offer spiritual sacrifices acceptable to God through Jesus Christ" (1 Peter 2:5).

The key to this spiritual offering is the work and dynamism of the Holy Spirit. This "priestly sacrifice" of daily life is more than simply the human effort of resignation to fate or the false denial of the true pain and cost of suffering. Rather, this aspect of lay spirituality reflects the constant effort to allow the Holy Spirit to open up avenues of understanding and spiritual resources needed to cope with the pains, losses, and tragedies of life. Yielding to the power of the Holy Spirit is how daily suffering can be joined with the sufferings of Christ in his redemptive work. Using the language of priestly worship, St. Paul urges Christians to consider the Christian life through this lens of a spiritual sacrifice. "Present your bodies as a living sacrifice, holy and acceptable to God, which is your spiritual worship" (Rom 12:1). Vatican II states that this can only be accomplished in the power of the Holy Spirit. In willing the lay faithful to continue his witness and service, Christ lets them share in his priestly function of offering spiritual wor-

ship. Any works that they carry out in the Spirit, even their sufferings patiently borne, become "spiritual sacrifices acceptable to
God through Jesus Christ" (LG 34).

The hardships of life can become opportunities to join in the
priestly work of Christ, who even now is bringing about the redemption of the world. This makes the laity cooperators in the reconciliation of all things to God. And this priestly offering of daily sufferings
is not an individual affair lived isolation from others; rather, it is
the activity of the whole church, the communion of believers,
who together offer sacrifice and praise to God. St. Paul even challenges believers to consider their sufferings in a kind of spiritual
solidarity with others in the Body of Christ. "If one member suf-
fers, all suffer together with it; if one member is honored, all
rejoice together with it" (1 Cor 12:26).

The Holy Spirit, the bond of communion with God and others,
is the source of this spiritual solidarity. This means that personal
sufferings can be offered up for the sake of the whole church. In a
mysterious way, the whole Christian community can receive spiritual graces when the sufferings of any one member of the Body are
united to the sufferings of Christ himself. St. Paul claims: "I am now
rejoicing in my sufferings for your sake, and in my flesh I am com-
pleting what is lacking in Christ's afflictions for the sake of his body,
that is, the church..." (Col 1:24).

The council does not "romanticize" suffering or make it into
some sort of "sign of God's favor," as some traditional spiritualities occasionally attempted to do. Instead, it faces the reality of
suffering head on and grounds it in the virtue of Christian hope.
Only from the perspective of Christ's Easter victory over sin and
death can believers have hope even amidst pain, hatred, meaninglessness, and loss. "Among the trials of this life they find
strength in hope, convinced that 'the sufferings of the present
time are not worthy to be compared with the glory to come that
will be revealed in us' (Rom 8:18)" (AA 4).

LOVE OF GOD AND LOVE OF NEIGHBOR

All of the spiritual helps and dimensions of lay spirituality
discussed above have as their aim the deepening of a relationship

with God and others through a life of charity. *Lumen Gentium* uses the language of love to explain this call: charity, the bond of perfection, is the supreme means of attaining holiness and guides us to our final end. Love of God and love of neighbor distinguish the true disciple of Christ and witness to holiness (LG 42). Christ himself taught that all of the commandments could be summed up in this twofold love.

> You shall love the Lord your God with all your heart, and with all your soul, and with all your mind. This is the greatest and first commandment. And a second is like it: You shall love your neighbor as yourself. On these two commandments hang all the law and the prophets. (Matt 22:37–40)

Love is the key to union with God and to the transformation of the world (LG 40). The holiness of the lay faithful flows into this life of charity, which can be characterized as their mission. And, at the same time, laypeople are sanctified and grow in holiness by the very activities that comprise this mission. Thus holiness is "a fundamental presupposition and an irreplaceable condition for everyone in fulfilling the mission of salvation within the Church" (CFL 17) and is the fruit of life according to the Spirit (cf. Rom 6:22; Gal 5:22). This Spirit-life enlivens each baptized person, calling them to imitate Christ in embracing the Beatitudes, meditating on the Word of God, participating actively in the liturgy and sacraments, in personal prayer, in their families or communities, in striving after justice, and in practicing the commandment of love in all circumstances, especially in service to the least, the poor, and the suffering (CFL 16).

Conclusion

The greatest challenge for lay spirituality is integration. The so-called "life of faith" must be integrated with "real life." There should be no dichotomy, therefore, between the faith life of the laity and their everyday activities, no divide between private devotion and public witness. *Gaudium et Spes* stated that such a split ought to be counted among the more serious errors of our time and called for an end to any false opposition between one's professional and social activities on one hand, and their religious life on the other (GS 43).

The life of charity is a daily challenge in the midst of the ordinary affairs of family, work, and society. According to the council fathers, this charity is to be lived chiefly in the ordinary circumstances of life and not only in important situations; God's Word revealed the new command of love to be the basic law of human perfection as well as of the world's transformation (GS 38).

The spirituality of the laity is one of involvement and engagement and not of withdrawal from the world for the sake of holiness. In big and small ways, the lay faithful are called each day to serve God and others through tasks and duties inherent to their lives in the world. And this is precisely how laypeople grow in their relationship with God. In fulfilling their secular duties in the ordinary circumstances of life, the laity "do not separate union with Christ from their life but rather performing their work according to God's will they grow in that union" (AA 4).

The secular character of the vocation and mission of the laity means, concretely, that lay men and women fashion their spirituality in the midst of the ordinary, the mundane, and the commonplace. They are challenged to allow God's love to shine through their ordinary service and tasks, whatever the duties and circumstances of their lives, so that they constantly grow in holiness and thereby manifest to all they meet the love with which God loved the world (LG 41).

This integration does not happen automatically; it must be taught and nurtured as the spiritual journey of the laity unfolds. An authentically lay spirituality must take fully into account the genuine obstacles and challenges to integrating faith and life. A formation is needed that is itself "integrated"; that is, the spiritual formation of the laity itself must take into consideration every area of their busy lives. For example, family life and work would have a special emphasis in such an integrated formation.

Pope John Paul II warned against placing faith and secular life in separate compartments and about the need for integration.

Every area of the lay faithful's lives, he pointed out, is part of the plan of God, who wishes these very areas to be the "places in time" in which the love of Christ is revealed and realized (CFL 59).

The pope's notion of "places in time" shows that it is really through ordinary human life and the things of every hour of every day that union with God comes about. Through spiritual formation, the lay faithful need to be sensitized to the fact that ordinariness and the messiness of the mundane can bring with them deep blessings. The challenge is to be trained to see the extraordinary in the ordinary, to attend to the sometimes hidden signs of God's presence in each day. God is to be encountered right in the midst of the hustle and bustle of life, not away from it. This simple yet profound insight can bring great freedom and joy into the spirituality of the laity.

Reflection Questions

1. In your opinion, why do many people today describe themselves as "spiritual, but not religious"?

2. Explain the spiritual dimension of the three offices of Christ as they apply specifically to the laity.

3. When has the "messiness of the mundane" been a source of spiritual growth in your own life?

4. What are some effective ways of forming a mature lay spirituality that can even embrace suffering?

5. Why is "work" often not included in the average layperson's understanding of spirituality?

Conclusion

Pope John XXIII prayed for a new Pentecost in anticipation of the Second Vatican Council. His hope was that the church would be gathered once again in an "upper-room experience" to receive a deep outpouring of the Holy Spirit that would stir the hearts of all believers. He prayed for a renewed church and a transformed world. And among all the members of the church, it seems that the laity have been the most affected by the wind and fire of the Pentecost power of the council.

During the now more than forty years since Vatican II, the lay faithful have been challenged to rediscover their vocation, mission, charisms, and spirituality in light of the renewed teaching of the council. The theology of the laity crafted by the council has had a profound impact on the identity and responsibilities of laypeople. No longer content with the old "pay, pray, and obey" model, the laity have taken their sacramental identities seriously. Baptism and confirmation reveal their vocation and mission in the church and in the world.

This book has attempted a simple explanation of the renewed theology of the laity. When compared with the traditional view of the laity, the teachings of the Second Vatican Council show a remarkable renewal of the identity and role of the lay faithful. The call to adulthood helped laypeople to realize their rightful role in the church. And the dismantling of the old power pyramid model of the church in favor of the communion model facilitated the process of lay men and women embracing their duties and responsibilities in the Body of Christ. Instead of a passive approach to their lives as Catholics, the laity were called to a much more active role in the mission of the church. And by stressing a more positive view of their temporal affairs in the world, the council enabled them to answer the call to holiness in their everyday lives.

Vocation

The council's description of the lay vocation moved away from the negative language that had traditionally described it. The concept of the laity as *not* clergy or *not* religious was replaced by a description based in baptism: The laity *are* the baptized members of the Body of Christ who share in the three offices of Christ as priest, prophet, and king in their own unique way. By putting baptism back into the center of its understandings of all vocations, the council removed any misperceptions that the lay faithful were somehow second- or third-class citizens in the church.

Secular Character

The focus on baptismal identity also ensured that the secular character of the lay vocation was not understood as a concession to "worldliness." Among the various members of the church, the laity have a distinctive share in the overall secular dimension of the entire church. Their distinctive secular character actually gives an ecclesial shape and meaning to their daily lives in the world as they fulfill their mission to be its salt, light, and leaven. They seek the kingdom of God precisely by engaging in these secular affairs.

Call to Holiness

The universal call to holiness was another important breakthrough in the teachings of Vatican II. The traditional perceptions of holiness were usually patterned on the examples of clergy and religious, their lifestyles thought to be the only true paths to sanctity. But by reclaiming the New Testament theology of baptism, the council provided a fresh appreciation of Christ's exhortation to every believer to grow in holiness. The ordinary lives of the lay faithful were not an obstacle to holiness, but rather opportunities to progress in the Christian life. Spiritual maturity for laypeople meant a conscious experience of union with God in daily life.

Mission

In the communion of the church, holiness is a source for mission. The graces of sanctification are spiritual fuel for bringing about the kingdom of God through word and deed. Christ himself calls and authorizes the laity for their mission in the church and in the world. The council taught that it was not the hierarchy alone who were entrusted with responsibility for Christ's mission; the laity are also summoned and equipped for the mission of the church through their baptism and confirmation. The gifts or charisms that are received through these sacraments are to be fostered so that the mission in the church and in the world can be fulfilled.

Ministry

This one mission of Christ has a diversity of ministries within it. Prior to Vatican II, it was common to associate the practice of ministry within the church only with the clergy. Any consideration of the theology of ministry focused exclusively on the sacrament of holy orders. By presenting the experience and teaching of St. Paul, however, the council affirmed that there was historical precedent for laypeople to be involved in intra-ecclesial ministry. St. Paul's notion of ministry as a collaborative endeavor, based on the charisms in the Body of Christ, shaped the council's teaching on lay ministry and the care of souls.

Crafting a theology of ministry to match the praxis of lay ecclesial ministry is an ongoing endeavor. This theological process is affected by dichotomies within the teaching of the council itself such as: "church and world," "sacred and secular," and "ministry and apostolate." These apparent tensions, however, can become the means for a creative and constructive approach to ministry. Indeed, the U.S. Catholic Bishops' 2005 document *Co-Workers in the Vineyard of the Lord* is an important source of teaching in this ongoing process. While remaining grounded in scripture and tradition, it attempts to respond to the contemporary phenomenon of lay ecclesial ministry since the council. *Co-Workers* treats the critical theological themes of vocation, sacramental identity, communion, charisms, secular character, and ministry in an effort to contextualize lay ecclesial ministry in church doctrine and teaching.

Lay Spirituality

Finally, the most important aspect of any theology of the laity is spirituality. Union with Christ in charity leads to a life long adventure of spiritual growth. The spirituality of the lay faithful is not meant to be a watered-down version of religious life but rather a robust, dynamic life of discipleship that fits their unique vocation and mission. Lay spirituality is not second best to that of clergy and religious; instead, lay spirituality takes daily life seriously as an opportunity to grow in holiness. There is no situation, event, duty, or experience that cannot be folded into the ongoing spiritual journey of holiness.

The Second Vatican Council did not offer an exhaustive teaching on lay spirituality, but it did provide some building blocks for crafting one. While the components articulated by the council are not specific to lay spirituality, they can be molded to fit their vocation and mission. The elements suggested by the teaching of the council include: the Word of God, the sacraments, prayer, charisms and virtues, family life, work, suffering, and love of God and neighbor. By intentionally engaging these elements each member of the laity can personalize the church's spiritual traditions and resources.

The spirituality of the lay faithful is shaped by their sharing in the three offices of Christ as priest, prophet, and king. Their priestly duties include the offering to God of hopes, dreams, joys, as well as sufferings and sorrows in an act of spiritual sacrifice for their own transformation and for the salvation of the world. As prophets, the laity are to allow the Word of God to dwell in them richly so that they might be witnesses of God's love to others. Their prophetic witness is in both word and deed and is grounded in the hope that is within them because of their union with Christ. Their participation in the royal office of Christ impels the lay faithful to master sin and order all of creation according to the shape and contour of the kingdom of God. They do this most fundamentally by allowing God to reign in their lives and then extending this reign by their actions, priorities, and testimony in the ordinary affairs of each day.

The Future

When the apostles and followers of Jesus received the Holy Spirit at Pentecost, they were gathered together in one place, praying with Mary, the mother of Jesus (Acts 1:13–14; 2:1–4). Mary had received the Holy Spirit in a profound way through her "yes" to God's plan at the annunciation and was therefore a fitting model of openness and receptivity to God (Luke 1:26–38). In her role as mother of the Christian community, she could teach them to follow the Spirit's lead and to be attentive to what new thing God was doing in their midst. Pentecost was, indeed, a new thing. The Holy Spirit formed the church and energized it for mission to the ends of the earth.

At Pentecost, the same creative power of God's spirit that hovered over the waters of chaos and brought forth life at creation (Gen 1:1–2) and later overshadowed Mary to bring about the conception of Jesus in her virginal womb (Luke 1:35) was present in a new way. Pope John XXIII prayed for this creative, life-giving power to be present in the church for the transformation of the world. More than forty years after the council, this Holy Spirit is still leading the church to understand, appropriate, and live the teachings of Vatican II. May Mary, the Mother of God, by her example and intercession, inspire all believers to be open to God's word and receptive to his grace.

> Let anyone who has an ear listen to what the Spirit is saying to the churches....The Spirit and the bride say, "Come." (Rev 2:7; 22:17)

Notes

Chapter One

1. Pope John XXIII, *Humanae Salutis* 23.
2. Second Vatican Council, *Gaudium et Spes*, The Pastoral Constitution on the Church in the Modern World, 43, http://www. vatican.va/archive/hist_councils/ii_vatican_council/documents/ vat-ii_const_19651207_gaudium-et-spes_en.html. Hereafter GS. Subsequent citations refer to this form of the document.
3. Second Vatican Council, *Lumen Gentium*, The Dogmatic Constitution on the Church, 41, http://www.vatican.va/archive/ hist_councils/ii_vatican_council/documents/vat-ii_const_ 19641121_lumen-gentium_en.html. Hereafter LG. Subsequent citations refer to this form of the document.
4. Second Vatican Council, *Apostolicam Actuositatem*, The Decree on the Apostolate of the Laity, 2, http://www.vatican.va/ archive/hist_councils/ii_vatican_council/documents/vat-ii_decree_19651118_apostolicam-actuositatem_en.html. Hereafter AA. Subsequent citations refer to this form of the document.
5. Second Vatican Council, *Sacrosanctum Concilium*, The Constitution on the Sacred Liturgy, 1, http://www.vatican.va/ archive/hist_councils/ii_vatican_council/documents/vat-ii_const_ 19631204_sacrosanctum-concilium_en.html. Hereafter SC. Subsequent citations refer to this form of the document.

Chapter Two

1. Pope John Paul II, *Christifideles Laici*, On the Vocation and Mission of the Lay Faithful in the Church and in the World, 9, http://www.vatican.va/holy_father/john_paul_ii/apost_exhor tations/documents/hf_jp-ii_exh_30121988_christifideles-

laici_en.html. Hereafter CFL. Subsequent citations refer to this form of the document.

Chapter Three

1. Second Vatican Council, *Unitatis Redintegratio*, The Decree on Ecumenism, 6, http://www.vatican.va/archive/hist_councils/ii_vatican_council/documents/vat-ii_decree_19641121_unitatis-redintegratio_en.html.

Chapter Five

1. *Gravissimum Educationis*, Declaration on Christian Education, 7, http://www.vatican.va/archive/hist_councils/ii_vatican_council/documents/vat-ii_decl_19651028_gravissimum-educationis_en.html.

2. *Ad Gentes*, Decree on the Church's Missionary Activity, 26, http://www.vatican.va/archive/hist_councils/ii_vatican_council/documents/vat-ii_decree_19651207_ad-gentes_en.html.

3. United States Conference of Catholic Bishops, *Co-Workers in the Vineyard of the Lord*, 6, http://www.usccb.org/laity/laymin/co-workers.pdf. Hereafter *Co-Workers*. Page numbers in subsequent citations refer to this form of the document.

Suggested Reading

Aumann, Jordan. *On the Front Lines: The Lay Person in the Church after Vatican II*. New York: Alba House, 1990.

Congar, Yves. *Lay People in the Church*. London: Geoffrey Chapman, 1965.

Coughlan, Peter. *The Hour of the Laity: Their Expanding Role*. Newtown, Australia: E. J. Dwyer, 1989.

Fox, Zeni. *New Ecclesial Ministry: Lay Professionals Serving the Church*. Franklin, WI: Sheed & Ward, 2002.

Graham, William C. *Clothed in Christ: Toward a Spirituality for Lay Ministers*. New London, CT: Twenty-Third Publications, 2007.

Hagstrom, Aurelie. "Laity, Theology of." In the *New Catholic Encyclopedia*, rev. ed. Vol. 8:290–93. Edited by Berard Marthaler. Washington, DC: Catholic University of America Press, 2002.

———. "Lay Ecclesial Ministry and Questions of Authorization." *Origins* 37, no. 7 (June 28, 2007): 107–10.

———. *The Concepts of the Vocation and Mission of the Laity*. San Francisco: Catholic Scholars Press, 1994.

Leckey, Dolores. *The Laity and Christian Education*. New York/Mahwah, NJ: Paulist Press, 2006.

Miller, Richard, ed. *Lay Ministry in the Catholic Church*. Liguori, MO: Liguori Press, 2005.

Orsuto, Donna. *Holiness*. London: Continuum, 2006.

Osborne, Kenan. *Ministry: Lay Ministry in the Roman Catholic Church*. New York/Mahwah, NJ: Paulist Press, 1993.

Philibert, Paul. *The Priesthood of the Faithful: Key to a Living Church*. Collegeville, MN: Liturgical Press, 2005.

Shaw, Russell B. *Catholic Laity in the Mission of the Church*. Bethune, SC: Requiem Press, 2005.

Wood, Susan, ed. *Ordering the Baptismal Priesthood*. Collegeville, MN: Liturgical Press, 2003.

Also in the Rediscovering Vatican II series

The Laity and Christian Education:
Apostolicam Actuositatem, Gravissimum Educationis
Dolores R. Leckey

This book tells the story of how the role of the laity—as essential in the life of the Church—moved to "center stage" during the Council, and how lay people were among those who made it happen.

0-8091-4220-1 Paperback

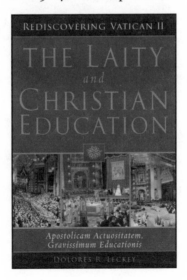

The Church and the World
Gaudium et Spes, Inter Mirifica
Norman Tanner

Traces the evolution, reception and likely future influence
of Vatican II's "key decree," *Gaudium et Spes*, as well as the
council's decree on the mass media, *Inter Mirifica*: its evolution
during the council and subsequent influence.

0-8091-4238-4 Paperback

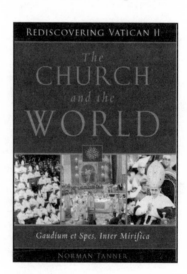

The Church in the Making:
Lumen Gentium, Christus Dominus, Orientalium Ecclesiarum
Richard R. Gaillardetz

The Church in the Making explores the teaching of three
documents from the Second Vatican Council on the nature of
the church, while also considering how that teaching has been
implemented in the last four decades.

0-8091-4276-7 Paperback

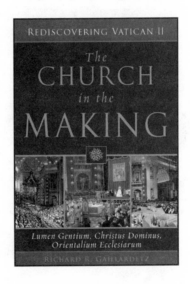

Scripture: *Dei Verbum*
Ronald D. Witherup

This book describes the history of the *Dogmatic Constitution on Divine Revelation*, its content, its importance, and how it has helped to direct the future of Roman Catholic biblical studies.

0-8091-4428-X Paperback

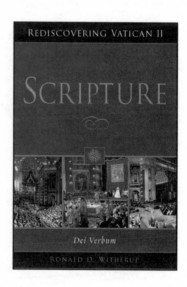

Ecumenism and Interreligious Dialogue:
Unitatis Redintegratio, Nostra Aetate
Edward Idris Cardinal Cassidy

An in-depth examination of the consequences for the
relationship of the Catholic Church with other Christian
churches and world religions as a result of the decisions made
by the Second Vatican Council forty years ago, and presented in
the documents *Unitatis Redintegratio* and *Nostra Aetate*.

0-8091-4338-0 Paperback

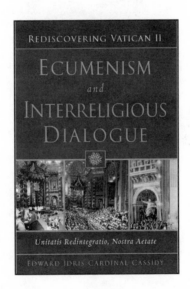

Liturgy: *Sacrosanctum Concilium*
Rita Ferrone

This book tells the story of The Constitution on the Sacred
Liturgy, presents and analyzes its main points, and describes
how its agenda has fared on its sometimes tumultuous journey
from the time of Vatican II up to the present.

978-0-8091-4472-3 Paperback

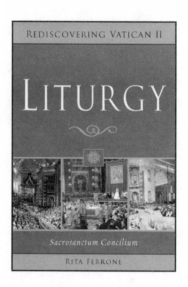

Religious Life and Priesthood:
Perfectae Caritatis, Optatam Totius, Presbyterorum Ordinis
Maryanne Confoy

Examines the historical context, the key players and the implementation of the Vatican II documents on priesthood, training of priests and religious life. It offers a contemporary vision for and critique of ecclesial ministries for the 21st century.

978-0-8091-4454-9 Paperback

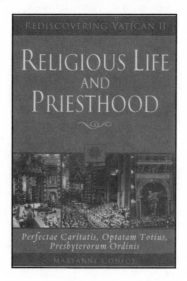

Spiritual Masters for All Seasons
Michael Ford
HiddenSpring

A blend of the spiritual and journalistic, this book explores the outer characters and inner convictions of the most inspirational figures of recent times.

978-1-58768-055-7 Paperback

Becoming Who You Are: Insights on the True Self from Thomas Merton and Other Saints
James Martin, SJ

By meditating on personal examples from the author's life, as well as reflecting on the inspirational life and writings of Thomas Merton, stories from the Gospels, as well as the lives of other holy men and women (among them, Henri Nouwen, Therese of Lisieux and Pope John XXIII) the reader will see how becoming who you are, and becoming the person that God created, is a simple path to happiness, peace of mind and even sanctity.

1-58768-036-X Paperback

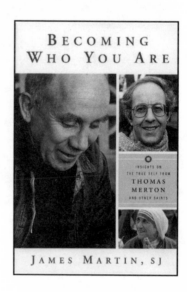

The Catholic Prayer Bible (NRSV):
Lectio Divina Edition
Paulist Press

An ideal Bible for anyone who desires to reflect on the
individual stories and chapters of just one, or even all, of
the biblical books, while being led to prayer though meditation
on that biblical passage.

978-0-8091-0587-8 Hardcover
978-0-8091-4663-5 Paperback

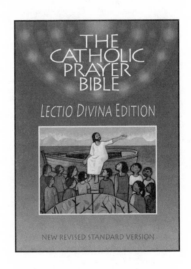